Handwoven Textiles
of
Early New England

The Legacy of a Rural People *1640-1880*

Handwoven Textiles of Early New England

Nancy Dick Bogdonoff

Stackpole Books

HANDWOVEN TEXTILES OF EARLY NEW ENGLAND

Copyright © 1975 by Nancy Dick Bogdonoff

Published by STACKPOLE BOOKS
Cameron and Kelker Streets
Harrisburg, Pa. 17105

Printed in the U.S.A.

Library of Congress Cataloging in Publication Data

Bogdonoff, Nancy Dick, 1928–
  Handwoven textiles of early New England.

  Bibliography: p.
  Includes index.
    1. Textile industry and fabrics—New England—History.
  2. Hand weaving—History. I. Title.
TS1323.15.B63   677'.02864'0974   75-5582
ISBN 0-8117-0783-6

Dedicated to my three sons—Paul, Peter, and Philip—
who know well the sound of the loom, and without
whose spirit of cooperation this book
would not have been written

CONTENTS

7

PREFACE

*M*UCH HAS BEEN written about the homes of the wealthy and the merchants' mansions of the New England seaport towns. Much has been said and documented about the exquisite imported harrateens, brocades, copperplates, toiles, and other textiles used in home furnishings. But little has been published to reveal both the dignity and diligence of the New England farmer and his wife in making their home. The farmer, after all, constituted the *majority* of the population of early New England. He could ill afford, nor was he exposed directly to, the luxuries of society and current trends from abroad. For this reason, perhaps, the farmwife's household furnishings in common everyday use are more purely American. Surely the homegrown, handwoven textiles were a melding of homeland tradition, toil of the new land, sheepraising, spinning, dyeing, and weaving—literally a woven heritage of New England perseverance and ingenuity.

We cannot forget the very special contribution to our heritage made by the hand skills of the New England farmer and farmwife. We must not allow the common American's achievements and skills to be ignored in the fanfare surrounding the restored dwellings of the once wealthy merchants and educated few.

The textiles of the provincial New Englanders were a visible link with their own traditional past. The traditions persisted for generations, accepting change slowly, and then only in what has been recognized as the uniquely honest and naive adaptations of styles and periods.

The very earliest colonies established in the 1600s were isolated by their initial sparseness of settlement and gross lack of communication, save with England. As the first meager settlements grew and more ships and people arrived, families ventured inland to stake off farms and clear their acreage. Small self-sustaining villages emerged as nuclei of outlying farms. Before 1730, four out of five men were farmers. Almost everyone farmed and had a trade besides. The economy of the New England village was one based on bartering, i.e., trading a skill for a commodity. A farmer might forge some pots or a farming tool in exchange for grain to augment his much-needed supply, so that villagers were strongly interdependent for special services or items. There was little reason to travel from village to village, or, for that matter, means of doing so. At first, narrow Indian footpaths were the only way.

The Yankee peddler, carrying small, otherwise unobtainable items such as needles, spices, and indigo dye on his back from the newly arrived seaport ships, was the first to make commercial contact with the farmer. He was a welcome sight, a bearer of little household necessaries, and brought news from the seaport, taverns, and other villages along the winding way. Later, when he could use roads and a well-stocked wagon instead of his backpack along the footpaths, he brought a wider selection from the seaports and many items of far-off origin to tempt the villagers. The inhabitants often bartered for a special purchase with extra wool, cheese, or tools. Eventually, more roads were built in the years 1776–1800, thanks to the many peddlers' demands. Still, the farming villages remained isolated and almost independent, as far as their basic needs were concerned. When in 1789 the first road map appeared, no one bought it or needed it. It was ahead of its time. In the 1780s New England had a large shipbuilding industry in the coastal cities of Portsmouth, New Hampshire, and Boston and Salem, Massachusetts, fish were exported, and molasses and spices imported from the West Indies. Nevertheless, the peddler still remained the inland farmers' main outside contact, and the primary source of trade for several generations. These small isolated towns helped create the village provincialism that persisted into the nineteenth century.

It is not hard to understand that the fashions and ways of England and Europe were very slow to be adapted to more suitable country forms on the New England farms. While examining the styles of the various periods it is important to remember that there were long time-spans of ten years to possibly a generation before a traditional form was changed for a "new way." Some textiles remained traditional; others evolved as the result of period, political, architectural, climatic, or stylistic influences. The quantity and quality of all handwoven textiles were ultimately limited by the size of the farmer's annual flax and wool crops, the farmwife's skills and creativity, and the amount of help received from the itinerant weaver in the manufacture of the woven article.

With the already growing national interest and regional pride in restoring and preserving early rural New England homes, and pride in our bicentennial, it seems timely to compile a guide to textile furnishings as a reference or base for one's own adaptations or study. How were the finished woven articles originally used; how were they fashioned; what were the techniques (the construction and sewing) used?

For ease of reference and sake of clarity, the different uses of textiles are described in separate chapters. Within each such chapter is pertinent historical background, documentation, original uses, colors, and how the items were constructed, with diagrammatic sketches. Photographs included throughout the book show original New England textiles in proper use in museums and historical restorations, wherever they substantiate a custom or usage.

Since this is the work of an independent researcher, undoubtedly there will be errors. It is hoped that those in authority will share their knowledge and notify the author of any such unintended or perhaps misguided information.

A word is in order about the sources of historical information used by the author in writing this book. The lack of substantial evidence in some areas forced us to turn, in addition to others' careful studies, to varied sources.

The probate court records of the New England counties containing wills of early settlers beginning as early as 1633 in Plymouth, Massachusetts are both fascinating and informative. Part of the law in 1633, requiring the drawing up of wills, stated that one month after a person died the will would be proved by the governor and council. It was ordered that "wills . . . be proved orderly before the Govr and Councell within one moneth after the decease of the testator. And that a full inventory duly valued would be presented with the same. . . ." The original wills have been transcribed and are available to be studied today in typewritten or book form, and are to be found at various historical institutions, libraries, and county seats.

The household inventories written at the time of will-making are invaluable sources for detecting information of validity. Since each head of a household was required by law to itemize all his earthly possessions, their value, and to whom they would be bequeathed, these records reveal what items existed when and where, and who owned them. Some descriptions are vague, some spellings amusingly phonetic. There are also lists that are methodically explicit, giving a careful list of items in every room in the house. If taken in total context, one can envision a whole room, a household, a family, even a way of life. By comparing inventories, one can assess the wealth of each family.

We can form a mental picture of possessions of the wealthy—books, imported silver, toiles, damasks, elegant furniture, and deeds to vast grants of land. The farmer sometimes listed only the necessary possessions with which to live through the seasons—sheep, geese, cows, farm equipment, cooking pots and utensils, beds and bed furnishings, and handwoven clothing. Frequently there were many offspring left to carry on or share the division of a farm.

For the purposes of this study, it is necessary to gloss over the inventories of the prosperous mercantile and other wealthy families of the seaport towns in order to look into the significant handiwork of the greater farming population. Those New Englanders who lived remotely and by their own resourcefulness, ingenuity, and tilling of the rocky New England soil are of primary interest.

One finds many different spellings of these old inventory words. In his day-to-day records the farmer might use a consistent lexicon, but when the occasion arose to make a will that required listing an inventory, he was faced with the problem of spelling a word often pronounced, but seldom put to paper. A neighbor might help with the difficult writing, and his version could be different still. Thus, many words were spelled phonetically, occasionally in a way that looks strange, but which allows us to pronounce the word as it was heard. Often its early Anglo-Saxon origin shows. In the excerpts from such records included in this book, we have retained the original spelling.

Many books published between 1640 and 1880 containing commentaries of the times and records, weavers' drafts, and old newspapers have been revealing sources. Of significant visual impact is the close examination of many of the precious few early originals in today's museum textile collections.

Documentary evidence surrounding a handwoven textile can make even a woebegone frayed piece of blanket come alive with historical credibility. Bits of information that dovetail can support its documentation. A dated letter describing or ordering an item, embroidered or woven initials and dates, tradesmen's records such as the itinerant weavers kept, town records of vital statistics, founding dates of fulling and spinning mills, household inventories, and other related factors help to document or give proof of provenance to an item.

These several sources have yielded, and hopefully will continue to yield, further information concerning early textiles. The surface has merely been scratched, and there is much more to be unearthed and investigated.

Perhaps the best testimony to the heavy use these homely textiles received is the fact that some were just plain "worn out" of existence, or were thought so ordinary as to have ended in the rag bag. The original handwoven textiles remaining, now in collections, are either well-worn and faded fragments, or specimens obviously well tended with frugality, sentimentality, and loving care by many generations of prudent New England savers.

The contemporary term "homespun" mistakenly leads us to think of roughly spun, dull-colored, and crudely woven fabrics. However, most originals seen for purposes of this study were made of expertly spun, brightly dyed, and evenly woven yarns. Considering the limits of the barn-frame loom, patterns were often imaginatively designed variations of a traditional homeland form. Even the simplest plain weave is proof of pride in workmanship and the practice of expert craftsmanship. A tattered fragment will reveal these truths and may, in addition, show us how a hem or loop was sewn, or some other technique of construction which is valuable to study. In good condition, or "family worn," they are important evidence of a desire not only for function, but also for color, design, and workmanship in which to take pride.

Photographs illustrate room settings with antique textiles at various museums. Specific textiles of interest are shown in closer views. All textiles in the photographs are documented as having been made in the New England states.

ACKNOWLEDGMENTS

THE CONTINUING RESEARCH for this book was made possible in part by an award from the New England Chapter of the National Home Fashions League.

I am grateful to Mr. and Mrs. Robert Miner of the Early American Society for the enthusiastic endorsement of my work.

Many historical societies, museums, and libraries were most helpful in providing books, documentation, and other valuable information. I am indebted to:

Mr. Thompson Harlow, Antiquarian and Landmarks Society, Inc., Hartford, Connecticut; Mrs. Gilbert R. Payson and Mrs. Martha Hassell, Essex Institute, Salem, Massachusetts; Mr. Eugene Dodd, former Director, Hancock Shaker Museum, Hancock, Massachusetts; Mr.

Thomas W. Leavitt, Director, and Joyce P. Messer, Merrimac Valley Textile Museum, North Andover, Massachusetts; Mr. Larry Salmon, Curator of Textiles, Museum of Fine Arts, Boston, Massachusetts; Mr. James Deetz, Assistant Director, Plimouth Plantation, Plymouth, Massachusetts; Mr. Arnold Gifford, Saconesset Homestead Museum, West Falmouth, Massachusetts; Mr. Sterling D. Emerson, Director, and Mrs. Eleanor Nowlin, Research and Education, Shelburne Museum, Shelburne, Vermont; Mr. Richard Nylander, Curator, and Mr. Daniel Lohmes, Librarian, Society for the Preservation of New England Antiquities; Mrs. Kathleen Newcomb, Director of Museum Shop, the late Paula Sampson Preston, who first encouraged me to write, and Jane Nylander, Curator of Textiles and Ceramics, all of Old Sturbridge Village, Inc., Sturbridge, Massachusetts; Mrs. Charles Dansie, Curator, University of Rhode Island Textile Collection, Kingston, Rhode Island; Miss Dorothy Vaughn, former Librarian, Portsmouth Public Library, Portsmouth, New Hampshire; Mr. J. Herbert Callister, Wadsworth Atheneum, Hartford, Connecticut; and Mrs. Irene Dodge, Director, and Mrs. Harold Boothroyd, Wenham Historical Society, Wenham, Massachusetts.

My thanks to the many generous persons who loaned me rare and out-of-print books and patiently waited their return, and especially to Miss Ruth Montgomery for the study of her handwoven heirlooms.

Thanks also to Dorothy S. Waterhouse of Waterhouse Wallhangers, Inc., 420 Boylston St., Boston, Mass.

My very personal thanks to June Mayo, retired librarian of the Topsfield Library, who went out of her way to assist me many times; Mrs. Ruby Benson, Librarian of Boxford Library, who also helped me obtain books, and to my friend Janet Greenman of Erie, Pennsylvania, who believed all along.

Warm and grateful thanks go to Marguerite Whitley May, who with great patience and accuracy transcribed my squeezed and scribbled pages of longhand into orderly typewritten manuscript.

chapter I

THE HANDWEAVING ERA

A BRIEF ACCOUNT of the rise and decline of the homespun era in the New England colonies will provide a grasp of the labor involved with harvesting and preparing the yarns used. The rural areas of New England for about 200 years used handwoven textiles primarily, but there were several types of weavers as well as the farmwife who were involved in this hand manufacture. It is important to know about them, their tools, and their methods of weaving.

The Beginnings and Progress of Colonial Handweaving

For the first two decades of colonial life the settlers slowly spread out from the seaport towns into the country along the coastline. Immigration and communication from England continued, and purchases of woolen and linen textiles from England and the continent were possible because of the frequently arriving ships. Along with the immigrants came new provisions. However, the immigration temporarily dwindled about 1640. By 1640 the early settlers were well enough established in the colonies to raise sheep and flax in order to gradually replace their imported clothing and household textiles with their own hand-loomed fabrics. The early Plymouth, Massachusetts Godbertson will of 1633 lists "1 peece of loomework." In 1640 the General Court of Massachusetts ordered that there be home manufacture of woolen and linen fabric, and also ordered an inventory to be taken of all available weavers, spinners, flax breakers, spinning wheels, and flaxseed. A price was paid for every yard woven of linen, wool, and cotton. Appointed inspectors would come to homes to decide how much would be paid per yard according to the quality of yarn and weaving.

In 1645 an accounting of all the colonists' sheep was ordered by the magistrate, and wool exporting from England was stopped. The colonists held dear their valuable sheep and, in turn, wrote to friends coming across the sea to bring their sheep with them. By 1660 there were supposedly approximately 100,000 sheep in the colonies. For their success, the colonists were penalized in 1656. By enactment of the Massachusetts Court each household was required to produce a quota of three pounds of spun cotton, linen, or wool every week for thirty weeks of the year, provided the household could produce the work of a "whole spinner." This quota of a "whole spinner" was based on the total spinning abilities within the household, including women, girls, and boys. Each member's skill was determined on the basis of a half or a quarter spinner, to total, hopefully, a "whole spinner." If the quota couldn't be met, a severe penalty of twelve pence was imposed for every pound not produced. A busy mother with young children quite naturally could not spin as much or for as long as an unmarried older sister or aunt, and so the latter was given the legal title of spinster and was thus occupied to help the family meet its quota.

The breeding of sheep, the processing of wool, and the spinning and processing of flax became the all-important endeavors of men, women, and children. Raising sheep was something that became common for many in New Hampshire in the seventeenth century as part of their existence. In 1659 Hercules Hunking, who lived on Star Island, an island off the coast of New Hampshire, and made his living from the sea, left in his will "three botes [boats] with fowar mein sails . . . and tow [two] and twenty sheep and nine honks [geese]." He signed his name with an "X"—"Harkles X Hunkings." Even meager listings of possessions, such as that compiled by Philemon Dalton of Hampton, New Hampshire, in 1656, would include at least two sheep: "2 yearling heffer called chery, one swine, and 2 shee." And John Huggins in 1670, also of Hampton: "2 oxen, 2 cowes, and one heifer . . . wth 16 sheep and lambs." Richard York of Dover, New Hampshire, "being well stricken in years but ripe in memory," left sheep and swine. John Scribner of Dover in 1674 lists "2 sheep and land in the ox pasture, calve pasture, sheep pasture." "Hee sheep" and "ewes + rams" also are frequently listed in many inventories.

There are references to looms in inventories, along with mention of the fulling mill in Rowley not many miles south, thus corroborating the home weaving of wool. In 1678 Thomas Ward of Hampton stated, "I doe give unto my son Thomas Ward all my implements of husbandry and my weaving gears to my wife and my son Thomas," the implication being that they would both be involved in the use of the loom and its equipment.

It is interesting to note that sheep raising and wool production were not only a New Hampshire enterprise, for in the years 1665 and 1690 the taxes in Rhode Island were paid not in money, but in wool.

IMMIGRATION OF PROFESSIONAL WEAVERS

The manufacture of home-woven textiles increased, aided by the interest of immigrant weavers who wove yarn brought to them by the spinners. The professional weaving immigrants were encouraged to set-tle in towns with the lure of up to thirty acres of land. A known profes-sional weaver by the name of William How settled in Chelmsford, Massachusetts in the year 1650. Ten years before a William Rix, weaver, of Massachusetts had contracted with plans to have a new house built. There is evidence of other professional weavers having settled in New

England at an early date. Much more is known about Tristram Coffin, Jr., the son of the first Tristram Coffin of Plymouth and eventually Nantucket. Tristram, Jr. married Judith Somerby in 1653 in Newbury, Massachusetts. Here he built a house and raised eleven children while plying the trade of merchant tailor. A day book beginning in 1689 lists his entries of large amounts of spinning and weaving necessary to his trade. Quantities of "cottun and woolun cloath," forty-five inches wide, were woven by him and his son Nathaniel. When this particular son of several married in 1693, he brought his wife home to live and raised eight children. The house, with its additions, still standing in Newbury, is now known as the Tristram Coffin, Jr. home. Descendants of his family and those whose names are in his account book—names such as Bailey, Little, Titcomb, and Noyes—still live in Massachusetts. Other professional weavers are referred to in chapter 2.

Earlier immigrants who had come from wool-producing areas in England spread their knowledge and went into serious business. Several such families of weavers who had immigrated in 1638 from a woolen district of Yorkshire, England resettled in 1643 near Ipswich, Massachusetts in Rowley and are credited with having started the first fulling mill for the cleaning of woolen cloth as it was taken from the loom, thus beginning, as others would, the specializations that attended handweaving.

A large immigration of over half a million non-English settlers occurred in the first quarter of the 1700s. Scotch-Irish immigrants settling in New Hampshire brought with them the skills and knowledge of flax raising, linen preparation, and spinning. A large group settled in Londonderry, New Hampshire in 1719, and others settled in Maine and Massachusetts. The demand was great for their fine linens and their skill with the small flax wheel. Various establishments of weaving manufacture were set up, employing the professionally trained weavers from England, Scotland, and Ireland and teaching weaving and spinning.

THE WOOL ACT OF 1699

The home-woven manufacture of textiles in the colonies alarmed the British government. The increased production of the colonists allowed them a beginning of export trade, which the British considered threatening to their own flourishing textile trade. Consequently, Parliament passed the Wool Act of 1699, which forbade the colonies to export any kind of wool.

A section from this legislative measure, with its many seventeenth-century terms for woven textiles, reads: "No wool fells, shortlings, morlings, worsteds, Bay or woolen yarn, cloath, serge, bags, kerseys, says, frizes, druggets, shalloons or any other drapery, stuffs or woolen manufactured what so ever, made or mixed with wool or wool flax, being the production of manufacture of any of the English plantations in America, shall be laden on any ship or vessel." Woven goods were not to be transported by horse or carriage. This did not discourage the colonists. It simply reinforced their production. By the early 1700s, sheep raising and home weaving, with the help of professional weavers, were sufficient to meet the colonists' own needs. English wool imports continued, but were no longer in the great demand they had once been.

WEAVING SCHOOLS

In 1705 Jeremiah Jackson set up a weaving school in Boston, Massachusetts. Nathaniel Potter, in the first quarter of the eighteenth century, set up shop in Lynn, Massachusetts. Daniel Oliver in 1718 provided financial support for a spinning school in Boston for all ages' spinning instruction. Rhode Island had looms that were producing for the trade. By 1750 linen production had a good foothold in Boston, and by 1752 a spinning school was reopened by John Brown in Boston.

The *Boston Gazette*, August 14, 1753, told of a sermon given on the virtues of industry by the Society for Encouraging Industry and Employing the Poor. That afternoon after the sermon, "300 spinners, some of them 7, 8 years old and several of them Daughters of the best families among us" lined up in three rows with their wheels and spun in contest. "Several thousand spectators assembled on this occasion." The following year in August the *Boston Gazette* announced that the managers of the Spinning School of Charlestown "give publick notice that they are ready to employ two good [professional] weavers."

EARLY NEW ENGLAND WEAVING BUSINESSES

Although home weavers continued to produce for their family and household needs, they were not totally dependent on their own weaving of flax and wool. Since professional businesses of weavers, dyers, and fullers were available in the seaport towns, or near them, the housewife could have part of the laborious processes done by the professional. However, in the more rural areas, the colonists began to spread and establish self-sufficient farms and villages. The labor involved in textile manufacture for the home was a cooperative family endeavor and continued for four or five generations to come, in the rural outlying areas of New England.

Since practically everyone farmed, the farming went along with another specialization available to the rural community to help economically. Often the weaver was one in the village who could supplement farming with weaving, besides providing textiles for the family needs.

Abbott Lowell Cummings writes of the Newell family living in Southington, Connecticut in the 1700s. They left records of such a weaving business, as well as farming and running a saw mill. In 1768, Josiah Newell raised his house. In 1791 he wrote in his day book:

Mar 1   Elnathan Norton Dtr [Debtor]
           to six pounds six oz. of flax
           to cloth for shoes and a knot of thread
May 16   to weaving 21 ¾ yards of linen cloth

In 1792:

July   to weaving ten yds of Bedtick

The largest amount of yardage woven was recorded in June of 1793:

to weaving 36 yards of linen Cloth

Most items were at least ten yards, and some were twenty or thirty yards long.

The Newells were known to have had flax fields and the linen cloth may or may not have been produced there, but was homespun. As was the custom, weaving was often paid with the labor of the customers. Josiah Newell lists credit given to neighbors for their help, "By one days work Breaking flax," "by Spinning," "By breaking 10 pounds of wool," and "By combing 7¼ pounds of wool."

Receipts for dye baths and dyeing instructions indicate that this, too, was part of the family's, or Josiah's, work. Some of his amusing dye language is included in the section on dyeing in chapter 2. Existing woven items thought to have been made at the Newell farm include linen towels, woolens, blue and white checkered linen, and possibly printed resist dye linen.

IMPROVEMENT IN SHEEP BREEDING

From the mid-1700s through the time of the Revolution, home weaving gained impetus. The sheep raising industry flourished throughout New Hampshire, Massachusetts, Connecticut, and Rhode Island. A Mr. Foster of Boston imported some Negrette Merino rams from Spain in 1793. In 1802 the same Mr. Foster received a flock of twenty-one rams and ten ewes at his Vermont farm from the American ambassador to Madrid. After eight to ten years of importing more Negrette Merino rams and crossing them with native American sheep, a new sheep bore what is now known as the superior quality of Merino type wool. It grew in coarse ruffles across the sheep's body. The Merino sheep craze spread over Vermont and into other New England states.

FLAX PRODUCTION

Flax was the other product needed for the weaving of durable linen textiles. It, too, took well to the New England soil and climate, producing fields up to an acre in size of the tall, blue-flowered plant. At this time New England must have had many a picturesque and pastoral scene, with sheep grazing near the house or in a rocky pasture, crops in neat rows, and a field of blue flax blossoming.

25

WOOLEN AND COTTON MILLS

By the late 1700s mechanical improvements such as clocks, hand tools, and plows were being manufactured in limited quantities in the towns and some villages. The year 1788 brought the first woolen mill set up in Hartford, Connecticut and a cotton mill in Beverly, Massachusetts. In 1790 Samuel Slater of Rhode Island was credited with setting up a water-powered mill for spinning cotton in Providence. Slater had worked in the cotton mills in England, but was not allowed to bring back plans. He carried the plans in his head and built duplicate machinery from memory. The mill spun cotton into yarn that weavers were able to purchase at the mill. For the first time weavers were free from the toil of preparing their yarn, and many professional weavers bought the cotton yarn. A few years later in 1813, Francis C. Lowell of Waltham, Massachusetts was responsible for the production of the power-driven loom, and spinning and weaving were done under one roof. Despite these industrial advances, the farmwife continued her labors of preparing most of her yarns and weaving. Only occasionally did she take advantage of mills if they were nearby. Because of the lack of actual cash, the farmers' families seldom had the chance to buy expensive yarns or imports. Spinning, weaving, and dyeing were still important household duties. One industrial factor that did help the rural production of textiles was the carding mills, introduced in the 1790s. The process of carding wool before it was spun was tedious work. Now the farmwife could take her clean wool to the carding mill and "fetch it home" all prepared for spinning. By the 1800s there were few rural homes that did not produce most of their family and household textiles. Most of New England, 90 percent of it, in fact, at that time was agricultural. The farmsteads knew little of the excitement, color, and fashion of the seaboard towns. The period from 1815 to 1865 was considered "the flowering of New England"—the time of the rural farmer, poor and independent, but self-sufficient and farmbound. Only the richest farmers had carriages for travel. Most farmers tilled and rotated about 10 acres of their total farmland, which averaged 100 acres. The typical farmer planted Indian corn, grains, vegetables, and maybe an acre of flax. He reckoned his small wealth not in cash, but in his land, livestock, farming equipment, and buildings.

The history of colonial handweaving spans some two hundred years until the Civil War in 1860. The farmers went off to war, leaving the women to care for the crops and livestock. Some home weaving continued in the remote upland areas of New England several years after the war. However, farming itself began to decline as early as the 1830s. The farming communities began to fade away, mill towns popped up, and other wage-earning industries beckoned to the young.

chapter 2

MATERIALS AND TOOLS OF THE WEAVING TRADE

The Yarns and Fabrics

LINEN

*T*HE FLAX PLANT from which linen is spun and woven is one of the oldest, and its natural fibers among the strongest known to man. Swiss lake dwellers used linen for fishing nets, the Egyptians wrapped their pharaohs and other mummies in it, and the Greeks wore togas of it. Linen has been woven and worn in many parts of the world for centuries and grown under a variety of climatic conditions. *Linum usitatissimum* is the botanist's name for flax, *usitatissimum* meaning "most useful." Indeed, it was a most useful plant to the colonists. They wove their finest table linens, bed sheetings, and personal underclothes from its longest and strongest fibers. Their more utilitarian textiles, such as grain sacks and towels, were woven of the not-so-fine tow linen. Its roughest outer fibers were twisted to make all sizes of cording and rope.

The plant itself was interesting, having a fairly small root system and a thin tall stem of twenty-four to thirty inches crowned by a group of small brilliant blue flowers. The stem contained the multipurpose fibers. There were layers of shorter tan and gray fibers surrounding the creamy-colored longest fibers in the center. The hard brown outer shield of the stem was discarded, then through repeated combings the gray tow fibers were separated from the long line fibers. The flaxseed was sewn early in the spring. A planned portion of the crop was allowed to go to seed, the seeds being saved for the next year's crop.

Would that all New England restoration villages could have their plots of flax—and a *retting pool*, as was common in all agricultural areas for many years. The blue of the fragile flowering flax is akin to the deepest blue of the sky directly overhead on one of those clear sunshiny days—a patch of errant sky, blooming on earth. The wafting breezes carry a subtle grassy fragrance of the blossoms. In colonial New England, flowering time was the breath of joy before the arduous tasks of linenmaking ahead.

Specifically, the processes from flax to linen are described below. It could take sixteen to eighteen months from the time the seed was planted until the fibers were spun for weaving. Other factors—weather disasters, illnesses of family members, pregnancies and births, and the success of the flax crop itself—intervened at times, further delaying the process. With a knowing eye the farmer decided just when the flax plant was mature enough to produce strong fine linen. The plants were hand-pulled by the roots, then spread in the field or in small, leaning stacks to dry. When dry, the seeds were removed by *rippling*, using coarse combs. The seeds were later crushed for linseed oil. The flax plants were then soaked in the water of a stream or pond; this was a *retting* process to soften and loosen the hard woody outer coating of the stalks. This retting was an important procedure as its type could influence the color and quality of the fibers. If there was no stream or pond available, *dew retting* was useful. The flax was spread on the grass and watered and turned every day until there was indication that the outer coating was beginning to decay but the inner fibers were intact. Dew retting was said to have "laid out until it looked as if it was thoroughly spoiled." This method was longer than others, but produced strong, gray linen fibers. *Still-water retting*, such as in a pond, had to be watched and tended, as too much retting could cause the fibers to be brittle. Brittle fibers would break on the loom. In a stream where water was moving, *running-water retting* produced a strong, pale yellow fiber. After retting, the flax was carefully spread out again to dry. When dry, the messy process of *breaking*, or *braking*, with a *flax-brake* was begun. This was basically a heavy plank on legs with a heavy, flat top hinged at one end of the plank. A handful of stalks was laid on the lower plank and the heavy top plank was raised by hand and slammed down on the flax stalks, breaking the woody coating.

Scutching was the scraping away of the broken outer pieces to expose the inner linen fibers. A good, strong flax breaker could hit the flax with one blow and almost at the same time pull the flax away. Sometimes the outer stalk was broken by an old method called *swingling*. A *swingle*, or *switchel*, was a long, narrow, flat, wooden, swordlike tool held in the hand. This was used to clean the flax by beating or scraping on a hard surface.

Next began the dusty *hackling*, or combing of the inner flax fibers a handful at a time. The *hackle* is often seen in antique shops still. It is a rather lethal-looking device. It is a block of wood with iron spikes about three or four inches high set into the wood. These spikes varied in different hackles as to their closeness of setting, and refinement of the spikes. The coarsest hackles were used first, in a combing action, pulling away the roughest tow fibers. The process of combing was repeated, changing the hackles and gradually working up to the finest and closest-set spikes, until there were just the long "line" fibers. The tow fibers were combed with coarser hackles, and not as thoroughly. Tow fibers were not as valuable as the long line fibers. They were spun and woven as weft, or filler, with the spun long line fibers as warp, into lesser cloth, but were not strong enough to be used for warp. The tow linen could not be spun tightly and because of short fibers would pull apart under tension. The long line fibers were the lightest part of the stalk, colored a silvery gray or pale "flaxen" yellow. "Line" linen in its natural state, and woven on the loom, was not pure white, but was used for table and bed linens and bleached after weaving. The woven articles were washed and dried on the grass again and again until they were "fresh white."

The finest and silkiest linens were produced from flax harvested before it had matured. If the crop was allowed to mature and the seeds ripened, the quality of the linen suffered.

Spinning was the next step, after the labor of dressing the flax, as above. The long line could be spun extremely fine; the tow was rougher and difficult to spin smooth. The spinning wheel used to spin flax was the small foot power *flaxwheel*. The spinner sat at the wheel moving one foot up and down on the treadle near the floor. The treadle kept the wheel turning and this, in turn, rotated the spindle. The unspun dressed flax was previously wound over the distaff and drawn from it as the spinner needed. The spinner would draw out the long fibers of the flax and the spindle would twist them as it turned, winding the spun linen onto the spindle at the same time. When spinning was completed, the spun linen was measured into skeins of yarn knotted and saved for the warping or weaving on the loom. Linen yarn on the loom was wiry, with a mind of its own. The web produced while weaving was open. Not until repeated washing did the linen cloth become soft. With repeated washings and use it became more beautiful.

Inventories sometimes list "hempen sheets," "sheets of hampen," and "brown linen." In 1806 Forsyth wrote in his *Beauties of Scotland*, "large quantities are . . . exported . . . in an unbleached state"; that is, under the name of "brown linen" or "green linen." This helps to identify the coarser weave of linens which were also home-woven and used. The hempen in early inventories referred to coarser spun, heavier weight sheets. The "brown linen" listed was undoubtedly linen ready for the many washings and drying in the sun to be respectably "fresh."

WOOL

Large amounts of wool were used in all households, and especially the rural home, where families spun their own wool and knew well the familiar bleating of their nearby grazing flocks. For centuries past the properties of the natural fiber wool had been respected, and it assumed great importance to the early settlers of New England for clothing and household textiles.

The earliest sheep were modestly endowed with wool, having little patches of wool on faces, legs, or bellies. Because of the vigorous climate that demanded sturdy little animals to survive, their sides and backs produced a rough, scratchy, short fiber wool. Homespun cloth prior to Revolutionary date was said to have had a "hard hand," its fibers being "coarse" and "short," and would never be any competition for English wools. However, with the importation of Merino sheep in Vermont in the 1800s, cross-breeding took place. The softer, longer Merino-bred wool was much sought after and eventually brought ridiculously high prices. These Merino bred with early New England stock vastly improved the quality of the previously coarse fleece.

One of the many accounts of wool showing its early importance was in the will of James Wall of Hampton, New Hampshire, in 1659. He wrote: "I give unto my daughter Sarah a horse coltt of this yeere and a peese of stuffe between them [two daughters] to make Each of them a Goune the stuffe is a peese of mixt stuffe of a sad culler." The seventeenth-century word "stuffe" referred to the coarser group of wools. The "sad culler" had nothing to do with mourning clothes, but rather indicated that through the dyeing process the wool had become a grayed or saddened color. "Mixt stuffe" was wool woven of yarn that had first been dyed two separate colors, carded to mix the colors, and spun before weaving.

In Portsmouth, New Hampshire, in the year 1694 the inventory of the estate of Mrs. Ursulla Cutt listed homespun woolen yardage in a chest of drawers as follows: "Twenty One yds & halfe of home Spunn woolling cloth."

Wool was spun and woven at home long after the 1860s, when linen spinning definitely had dwindled. During the late seventeenth and through the eighteenth centuries the household surplus of wool was always a readily salable commodity for trade and barter.

It is not hard to understand its uses and demand. The properties of wool that we take for granted were essential considerations in the planning and weaving of wool fabric for a given use. Under today's microscope, the single wool fiber is seen to be made up of scalelike cells that overlap. These contract and expand and give wool its ability to return to form, or its resiliency. Over these scales there is a covering film of wax, which gives wool its water-repellent qualities. It is also flame-resistant—an important factor in the colonial home, where the hearth and candlelight were an ever present fire hazard. Wool also has the unique ability to both shed moisture and absorb it, protecting the wearer from sudden chills. The colonists found its wearing qualities numerous and long-lived for warm bedding. Since each fiber stands apart from others, a woven wool blanket could be light in weight, even if bulky, and filled with tiny air-capturing pockets of warmth. Its uses for outdoor clothing were obvious. Wool also dyed well, producing some of the brightest and lasting colors for household, clothing, and embroidery use.

Wool was and is enjoyable to handle while spinning and weaving. On the loom its accommodating fulling, or "filling in," properties allow the use of varying weights or thicknesses of yarn in the interlacement of warp and filler yarns. The other natural fibers, such as cotton and linen, require specific sizes or thicknesses of filler yarn woven with a particular weight warp yarn to produce a given fabric, whereas what might seem too open an interlacement of all-wool yarns on the loom could, after fulling, produce a coarsely woven but warm woolen textile. Even the youngest spinner's wool was worthy of weaving.

The uses of woolens in the household were many and varied from earliest times: "Red blancket for a child," woolen hangings for beds, underblankets, sheeting, plaid and check blankets, bed rugs, overshot patterned coverlets, woolen quilts, counterpanes, upholstery, cushion covers, window curtains, hooked rugs, and carpeting. The lesser unspun fleece of wool was used for quilts, pillows, cushions, and "flock" mattress fillings.

Wool processing began with the farmer's caring for and breeding of his sheep that grazed on his farmland or sometimes on a common grazing lot. In rural areas the early signs of spring meant getting ready for the sheep shearing. Sheep had to be washed first to remove the excesses of mud and other dirt from their wool. Usually a rushing stream on a mill dam was the chosen site, and often farmers worked together helping to gather the flocks in a pen for the purpose. One by one they washed the struggling sheep under the falls, then let them loose to dry in the sun and breezes before shearing. This was a traditional method shown in early European and English genre paintings and depicted on European and English printed textiles of the eighteenth century. The shearing of the sheep took considerable skill so that the sheep's hide was not cut. Although the shearing was done by a competent farmer, sometimes a professional sheepshearer traveled from farm to farm. His skills were learned in the wool-raising districts of England, enabling him to shear a great number of sheep a day.

The fleece, or sheared wool, was usually washed by the farmwife in a mild lye solution to further clean the wool of its impurities. This washing process was called scouring and was followed by spreading out to dry thoroughly. Then the fleece was picked to remove burrs, tags, and any other clumps of foreign matter not removed by scouring.

When carefully picked, the fleece was ready to be *carded*. *Wool cards* were slightly oblong flat pieces of wood with a side handle. The flat wood was angled slightly to the handle and facing upward on it were closely set wires similar to that on a dog's brush. Two wool cards were used, one in each hand, to separate and comb the wool fibers repeatedly until they were smooth and parallel. Then the wool was fluffed off the card, leaving it in a soft, airy-roving form called *spinning rolls*. Evidence of the prolific use of wool cards throughout New England was the significant production of 63,000 cards by a Boston firm in 1788. Some twenty years later carding mills, powered by streams to turn the necessary overshot wheels, sprung up in towns throughout New England. Now the farmwife could deliver her fleece and pick up the carded wool in spinning roll form for a small price. If she was not close enough to a town carding mill, she continued carding by hand. The spinning rolls were set aside in baskets until spinning time.

Spinning wool was done in an alternately standing and walking position, not sitting, as at a linen wheel. The wool wheel was very large and had no foot treadle to keep the wheel turning. The spinner stepped forward and back in a rhythmic motion. She had to alternately keep the wheel going and draw out the wool fibers from the spinning roll with one hand. With the other hand she held the spinning roll and manipulated it as it twisted and then wound spun yarn onto the spindle. Feed-

*The keeping room of the Richardson house at Old Sturbridge Village, where the added-on lean-to of the saltbox provides a long multipurpose room. The room appears much as it did in the late eighteenth and early nineteenth century. Cooking was done at the hearth to the right. The settle provided a shield from the cold and warmth near the fire—and, perhaps with a blanket, accommodated an unexpected overnight guest. The spinning wheel is placed near the window where good light was needed. Prepared rovings hanging from the side are ready for spinning. The bedstead at the end of the room is folded out of the way until nighttime, with bedding on it unnoticed and accepted in the daily routine. Floors are sand-scrubbed clean and bare. The sheathing is painted mustard.—*Old Sturbridge Village photograph by Donald F. Eaton

ing the yarn onto the spindle brought her in close to the wheel; the drawing out of the fibers required stepping back. Many miles were walked in a day by the spinner. The rhythm was often accompanied by a song or hymn. Mr. Samuel Goodrich, born in 1793 in Ridgefield, Connecticut, wrote in his childhood recollections about the spinning of wool. "The wool was also spun in the family partly by my sisters and partly by Molly Gregory, daughter of our neighbor, the town carpenter . . . In her solitary operations aloft, I have often heard her send forth from the attic windows, the droning hum of her wheel, with fitful snatches of a hymn."

After spinning, the wool was measured by transferring the yarn from the fatly wound spindles onto the *reel*. Basically the reel consisted of crossed wooden arms with yarn holders on each of the four ends. The crossed arms or reel were placed on a stand, allowing the reel to pivot to wind off the spindle yarn. The reel had a circumference of approximately six and a half feet. Some reels, called *clock reels*, had gauges that ticked with each rotation on a simple wooden dial. The count of revolutions was recorded and would show when the required measurement was wound. A *knot* was wound when the count registered forty threads or rounds. This was tied to mark and the winding continued, each forty rounds being tied until there were ten knots, or a *skein*. This was a consistent form of measurement from generation to generation. In 1875 Temple and Sheldon wrote in their *History of Northfield, Massachusetts* that "a knot was composed of forty threads, and a thread was 74 inches in length, or once round the reel." Yardage needed for warping the loom and also for the weft was calculated from these skeins. Wool spinning in rural areas continued long after weaving ceased and was used regularly for knitting yarn. Skeins also provided easy handling in dyeing and drying dyed yarns.

Because of the natural oils or lanolin in wool that helped both its water-repellent and wearing qualities, woolen fabric was often taken off the loom and used *undressed*, or unwashed When washing of the fabric was desired, the process of *fulling* removed the oils and helped the oilspun fibers to separate. The releasing of the oils allowed the fibers to expand and "bloom." The colors were also brighter after the removal of oils. This fulling process is sometimes misnamed "shrinking" because of the thickening and filling-in that occurs. Soap or soda was a common home means of fulling. The woven fabric was placed in a large tub with the soap or soda and trod upon with bare feet to help squeeze out the oils. It was a slow, messy, and tiring procedure requiring removal of soil, oil, and soap with numerous rinsings. Mills that were powered by forceful falls were known to have started commercial fulling as early as the late 1600s. By 1790 fulling mills were very common and a great help to the weavers, who simply took their woven woolen textiles to the fuller and let him do the heavy fulling work. The term *fuller's earth* comes from the early fuller's trade. It was a fine claylike pumice used to absorb the oils in the fabric and then washed out. Revolving paddles in tubs turned by the water-powered turbines made fulling a big business, which eventually incorporated dyeing as well. The fulling mill was a boon to professional and home weaver alike.

LINSEY-WOOLSEY

Linsey-woolsey was a finely woven material with lengthwise threads (warp) of handspun linen, across which handspun woolen yarn was woven. Both linen and wool were of single strand (ply) each, not doubled or tripled as woolen knitting yarn is today. This resulted in a closely woven, very durable and multi-purpose fabric that was used for household textiles as well as wearing apparel. The natural properties of moth-resistant linen (did you ever see moth holes in linen?) protected the wool. Together, these natural fibers created a mothproof, warm, and lightweight material. In the household it was dyed for bed hangings, coverlets, and upholstering and usually left natural cream for curtains, blankets, and sheeting.

COTTON

Cotton was imported from the Indies in the seventeenth century, but was mentioned in inventories usually in the context of knitted wearing apparel, such as stockings. It was shipped in its raw state, as picked directly from the plant. In this form it was known as *cotton-wool*. It had to be picked free of its seeds and was then spun into yarn. Because of the cotton's short fibers it was not strong enough when spun to be used for warp yarns. It was woven as filler on a linen warp until the close of the eighteenth century. Machine-spun cotton was not available much before the 1790s. This is not to say that cotton yard goods were not available. The *Boston Gazette* advertised imported "India dimities, cotton checks, chinces, callicoes, muslins, white callicoes, blue callicoes." But these were imported for the wealthy trade. The cotton-wool spun at home was often "mixt" or spun with wool for stockings. Knitted stockings persisted for over 150 years.

In 1796 the production of cotton in the South increased to thirteen times that of 1793, because of Eli Whitney's invention of the cotton gin. One gin or machine did the work of separating the seeds from the cotton that formerly took fifty people. The machine was so basic that it was copied everywhere. Prior to this time the South's cotton production was taken almost exclusively by England for its texile manufacture. The new cotton gin brought about the spinning and weaving of cotton in New England and added to the competition against English production. About this same time, Samuel Slater, who was an Englishman, left England for America with plans committed to memory for building cotton-spinning machinery. In Pawtucket, Rhode Island, in 1790, the firm of Almy and Brown, where Slater was now employed, opened the first duplication of the English spinning mill. Thus, Samuel Slater, with his fine memory, was credited with the beginnings of textile spinning and manufacture in America. It was very successful and afforded weavers, both home and professional, the opportunity of purchasing evenly spun, machine-manufactured cotton yarns for their use. The tedious processes of linen preparation could now be eliminated. After the 1800s, many handwoven overshot patterned coverlets, rugs, and utilitarian fabrics were woven using mill-spun cotton warp, and homespun, home-dyed woolen weft yarns. Linen tablecloths and linen bed hangings were now outmoded in favor of the newly desirable woven cotton ones. As with many of the "new" fashions, the remote agricultural communities continued with raising flax and preparing it, but cotton was nevertheless available for the home and professional weavers.

The Dyes

Although American Indians had knowledge of natural dyestuffs, the early colonists of the seventeenth and eighteenth centuries relied mainly on the traditional home dyeing methods learned in Europe, England, and Scotland. Some of the dyestuffs, such as woad, saffron, and madder, had been used for centuries before. A good many of the colonists' dyestuffs were found around them in the fields and forests of New England. They purchased those they could not otherwise obtain—indigo, fustic, turmeric, and cochineal—either from a peddler or the village store.

Various colors could be produced from the same dyestuffs by combining with different mordants. The mordant was the agent that chemically "opened" the fibers of the yarn, so to speak, to receive the dye and hold it permanently. The mordant was put into the dye pot to set the color already imparted to the yarn by the dyestuff. A dye that would run when washed was said to "bleed." A dye that would fade from exposure to light, soap, or alkali was called "fugitive." It was, therefore, necessary to choose the proper mordant to prevent fading, bleeding, washing out, or harshness to the yarn. Some of the mordants most frequently found in recipes for dyeing were alum, copperas, iron shavings, verdigris (rust of copper), cream of tartar, potash (wood ashes), chamber lye, and *aqua fortis* (nitric acid).

The following are either native or imported dyes known to have had popular usage in home dyeing into the mid-1900s:

COCHINEAL

This imported dye gave beautiful pinks, rosy scarlets, and crimsons. Although available to those who could afford it in seventeenth-century England, and exported at the time, cochineal was not commonly used in rural areas until well into the eighteenth century, and then it was still expensive—over twice the price of indigo. In 1831, a dye manual lists cochineal at a price of $.31 to $.375 per ounce, whereas indigo was $.14 per ounce. Its continued high price was due to the fact that the dye was derived from an insect that fed on a South American pear. It took 70,000 dried insects to produce one pound of cochineal. Bought in small quantities and used sparingly for the finest woven items, it was found at the village store. The less expensive madder dye was used for most household reds.

FUSTIC

Fustic, another imported dye, produced a deep strong yellow and was used in place of costly saffron (crocus pollen). It was employed in seventeenth-century England and became commonly used in the colonies in the eighteenth century. It was imported in logs, and was known as "dyers mulberry," being a tree of the mulberry family that grew in

South America and the West Indies. The logs were chipped into small pieces and tied in small sacks before entering the dye bath. Fustic was extensively used in dyeing colors such as yellow, drab (yellow-brown, khaki), olive, and green.

GOLDENROD

This natural dyestuff produced a yellow with clarity and fastness. It was known and used by home dyers in seventeenth-century England, as well as by colonists later.

HICKORY

This was a natural dye. The wood gave a yellow dye, the nut a brown dye. Sometimes home dyers used the wood as a substitute for turmeric or fustic.

INDIGO

Early in the seventeenth century in England, indigo was found to be an excellent replacement for woad, the earliest known dye for blue. In eighteenth- and nineteenth-century New England, indigo was the most popular, foolproof dye used. It produced all degrees of blueness, depending on how long the yarn was left in the dye bath. The colonists imported it from Bengal, the East Indies, and South America. It was a pressed powder from the indigo plant (*Baptisia tinctoria*), which had been cut at maturity, steeped, and fermented to produce indigotin. The indigotin solution was oxidized by paddles beating in air, the indigotin settled, the excess liquid was drawn off, and the remaining indigotin pressed, cut, and dried to be sold. The dark blue two-inch cubes were known as "junks." There were varying degrees of quality of indigo. The best was imported. A lesser quality was raised and processed in the Carolinas and New Orleans. This was harder and with more impurities, so that the quantity output was less. Indigo in all forms nevertheless possessed excellent color-fastness and color control properties.

Indigo dye was bought frequently at the village store in large amounts. The peddler was also a ready source of supply for dyeing. A farmhouse had its dye pot near the fire, where the indigo cubes had been placed to ferment, with bran, copperas, or even urine acting as a reducing agent. When the liquid "blue vat" or "blew pot," as it was called, was in soluble form, it was dissolved in an alkali solution. It was now ready to dye cloth, although the blue color was transferred to the textile after the latter had been submerged for a given period and then removed from the dye vat. When the air hit the indigo, oxidizing took place, making it then become blue.

The evidence of grades of indigo and other dyes and mordants and the sale of "blew pots" appeared in an advertisement in the *Boston Gazette*, March 5/12, 1739: "To be sold at the cross'd Pistols in Fish Street, by Obadiah Cookson . . . the very best Indigo, Figg-Indigo, Red-wood, Log-wood, salt-Petre, Allum, Copperas, Brimstone, Rosin . . . cotton wool, wool cards by Groce or Dozen, card-wire, Blew Melting pots."

MADDER

Madder was a natural dyestuff producing a reddish brown and reds. Its age was ancient. According to Rita J. Adrosko of the Smithsonian Institution, red cloth, very evidently madder-dyed, was found on Egyptian mummies of a predynastic era. It was made from ground-up tree root. Some madder was home-grown, but most came from Virginia. It was a staple red dye for wool and cotton by the eighteenth century. Some madder was imported from France and Holland. The extract of madder root could be purchased from the peddler. Fresh madder was twice as potent as the dried root. When the dye was made at home, the fresh root had to be beaten into a paste twelve hours after it was washed, and used right away to get the benefits of its potency. The colors could be reddish or brown, depending on the mordant chosen. Later, small amounts of cochineal were added for brighter reds.

REDWOOD

For brilliant red of "first rate color," one-half pound of redwood was needed, whereas one-fourth pound of redwood dye produced more "common color" red.

SASSAFRAS

Natural dyestuffs from the sassafras tree produced several colors. Yellow dye was derived from the wood, the bark of the root produced a brownish pink, and the bark of the tree was used for graying when nutgalls were not available. The leaves of this useful tree produced a flavorful tea. It had been known in seventeenth-century England and was used in New England where sassafras trees were found.

SUMAC

A natural dyestuff was obtained from sumac, a shrub considered native to America, but which had a European counterpart that was actually superior. Its stalks were used in the eighteenth century to make yellow dye, while drab (yellowish brown) and gray dyes were extracted from the shoots and leaves. Its berries yielded a gray color.

TURMERIC

The ground tuberous root of the turmeric, or Indian saffron plant, gave a rich yellow. It was considered the finest yellow not requiring a mordant. However, it was a fugitive, or not lasting, color; thus it was used mostly with other dyes to make browns and olive greens.

VERDIGRIS

This dyestuff was made in France from the rust of copper. It was used for dyeing green, chrome, and black.

WOAD

Woad was a blue dyestuff of ancient use. Caesar wrote that "all Britons stain themselves with woad, which gives them a terrible appearance in battle." Woad is thought to have been the first blue dyestuff used in America, and had been well known in Europe before the discovery of indigo in the late sixteenth century. In the seventeenth century indigo's value was evident, and by the eighteenth century indigo, easily obtained from the West Indies, had largely replaced woad. Most woad that was used earlier was imported from France and Holland. Some was grown in New England, but although growing was easy, the processing and fermentation were difficult. Woad could produce brilliant blues: the early young leaves yielded a light bright blue, the mature leaves a deep dark blue, and the well-ripened leaves a bluish black.

WOODS OF LOCAL TREES

Woods were chopped into small pieces or shavings and put into small tied bags before entering the dye bath. This protected the yarns and textiles from snags. Some common woods and the colors they produced follow.

Butternut Bark: Rich tans and browns, often used for home-dyeing yarns. Sometimes used for dyeing stockings a "tolerable black."

Camwood: Tones of plum and brown.

Hemlock Bark: Reddish brown.

Hickory: Yellow (from the wood), brown (from the nut). Sometimes home dyers used the wood as a substitute for turmeric or fustic.

Logwood: Used extensively in dyeing blacks and altering the shades of other colors. Logwood is history's most tenacious natural dyestuff.

Maple Bark: Produced a cinnamon brown when used with alum mordant.

Combinations of ingredients, both native and imported, were used and jotted down in receipts. Late eighteenth-century colors were arrived at laboriously. Olive green was the result of combining oak bark, alder bark, fustic, sumac wood, and copperas. A warm golden brown called snuf was made with butternut bark, fustic, redwood dye, and copperas, saddened (grayed) with butternut liquor. Walnut hulls and butternut bark, used together, would produce brown or dark brown without the use of a mordant. Nutgalls (formed by insects) and alder bark had a high tannin content, and were used together for dyeing black, after the material had already been dyed blue. The resulting blue bath from boiling bayberries for their wax in candlemaking was sometimes used with walnut hulls or bark for black dye; with copperas, the blue bath yielded brown dyes.

A specific type of cochineal known as "quicksilver cochineal," used with *aqua fortis*, produced a scarlet. Quicksilver or grayed cochineal was the result of the method used for drying the insects. If sun-dried, they stayed red; if dried by stove heat, they turned gray.

Blue Resist Dyeing

Shades of blue indigo, usually a medium blue and a darker royal blue, were used for printing on homespun linen for bed curtains and quilt covers in the late 1700s. Although blue resist dyeing was not as common in the rural areas as in the cities where professional printing was done, the housewife either took her own homespun to the printer or printed it herself. Some enterprising women advertised that they stamped linen in "china blue or deep blue." The printing was thought to have been done by hand blocking in a technique called "resist" or "discharge." Before printing, the background white linen (and wherever white was part of the design) was coated either with wax or clay. Then the blue designs were block printed. When printing was completed, the resist wax, which had not allowed any blue dye to penetrate the white ground, was removed by heat. If clay was used, this was washed out. Usually these designs were quite bold, with large overall patterns. They were often graceful and vital modified versions of the basic "tree of life" pattern, or certain motifs from it, such as oak leaves, acorns, flowers, birds, strong curving branches, and pineapples.

In spite of newspaper and inventory documentation unfortunately little original early blue resist exists that can be substantiated as having been printed in New England on home-woven textiles.

The Weavers

HOME WEAVERS

Weaving at home was carried on from the mid-1600s for generations in a great many country households of New England. Although factory-woven textiles were available in the cities in the early 1800s, the agricultural communities still raised their own sheep for wool and flax for linens into the 1850s. Even in the late 1800s, as pioneers moved westward out of New England, the homespun know-how produced the necessary clothing and bedding for the settlers. The mechanics of yarn preparation and weaving were firmly ingrained in their bodies as well as minds. They needed only recipes for dyeing and threading drafts for pattern weaving. Thus generations of family textile traditions were perpetuated.

Throughout the daylight hours working at the loom, or other weaving preparations, was part of the daily farmhouse routine. Early in childhood, daughters learned from their mothers and grandmothers how to throw the shuttle, beat the web just firmly enough, wind the bobbin smoothly, help with dressing (or warping) the loom, and spin and dye wool and linen yarns. An experienced weaver could weave five or six yards of cloth per day, once the loom was warped. If very carefully planned and meticulously calculated, warping the loom with many yards of fine strong linen would prepare it for weaving many different household textiles. By using varying thicknesses and colors of yarn in the shuttle, the weaver could plan sheeting, coverlets, table linen, striped ticking, linsey-woolsey blankets, and petticoats. There was always something in the large farming households that needed replacing, and a new coverlet pattern with which to experiment when time allowed.

In some households young boys were put to work winding spools for warping and bobbins for shuttles. They also helped with carding the wool before it was spun. Generally, the farmwife and her daughters, single aunts, and grandmothers were responsible for the spinning, dyeing, and weaving chores; while the men and boys took care of the sheep and sheep-shearing as well as raising and harvesting the flax crop. The crude spikelike combs called *hatchels* used by both men and women in

45

the shared hackling process held special significance for some young persons about to be married. So much a part of their lives was this total process of raising and tending the flax crop for the spinning and weaving of cloth, that the hatchel itself was thought by some to be an appropriate engagement or courting gift. It was a symbol of the unity of the sexes that otherwise had traditionally separate chores on the farm.

Some of the more proficient weavers were able to weave extra yardage for selling or barter. A woman living in Windham, New Hampshire, in 1817 was widowed with six sons and two daughters. She used her weaving skills to support her family by selling household textiles in Salem and Danvers, Massachusetts. Women in such circumstances put their families to work assisting in the weaving and warping of the looms. And together they worked at raising and preparing wool and flax before the process of weaving could even begin.

Early evidence of families weaving the wool and flax raised and prepared on their farms is scarce today. Thanks to the frugality, care, and knowing respect of their many descendants, a precious few of the textiles have been documented.

The Copp family, who settled in the late seventeenth century in the Stonington, Connecticut area was prosperous enough to afford some printed and imported textiles. Nevertheless, like many farm families, they wove great quantities of household fabrics. An extensive collection of both their purchased fabrics and many yards of home-woven textiles are now in the possession of the Smithsonian Institution. The presumed home-grown, homespun, and handwoven table and bed linens are numerous, as well as furniture check bed hangings requiring some fifty yards of material for the set. There are also a variety of handwoven coverlets, along with plain white homespun bed hangings. The total collection was woven from 1750 to 1850 and is further evidence of the enduring traditions in the household textiles that changed little over a century in providing basic fabric needs.

In 1668 William Gifford, a weaver, moved from Sandwich, England and received two grants for the coastal farmland on the cape known as the Saconesset Homestead. The early house is no longer standing, but the present ship's-bottom roof house, built in 1750, is owned by a descendant, Mr. Arnold Gifford. The homestead has the unique history of having had ten generations of Giffords farming it. Mr. Arnold Gifford says that his early ancestors were wool producers, weaving broadcloth. There were sheep on the farm until 1840, when the laurel bushes flourished out of bounds and took over the grazing land. Today sheep are again grazing at the homestead. They forage on grass through the winter on the cape, where the winters are a little milder than in the rest of New England.

Inside the house, along with generations of furniture, are hand-woven, handspun and dyed woolen coverlets and blankets, bedding, and clothing woven on the loom still occupying space in the loom loft. The linen was raised from flax, prepared, spun, and woven on the homestead. The articles have been used and cared for and saved by generations of Giffords. Two are illustrated in this book on pages 102–3.

An example of the singular industry of one woman who did all the dyeing, spinning, and weaving of yarns from sheep and flax raised on her farm in Stark, New Hampshire is pictured in the coverlet and blanket made by Dulcena Dewey shown on page 102 and 104. Descendants Ruth Montgomery and her brother tell of her spinning and dyeing wool from sheep grazing on the rocky pastureland surrounding the small farmhouse. "They were not poor. His work was good and they didn't want for anything. But Dulcena lived on a rocky farm. Could raise only vegetables, land so rocky only livestock they kept were sheep. She had to make do or do without. She did all spinning, dyeing, and weaving." Dulcena wove all the blankets, coarse linen for bed-ticking, summer blankets, colorful striped winter blankets, and a striped baby blanket for a particular baby, Oscar Montgomery, brother of Miss Montgomery. Also woven by Dulcena Dewey was a coverlet of expertly dyed black and butterscotch-colored handspun yarns. Miss Montgomery, who was seventy-three in 1971, said the coverlet was used by her grandfather and taken to "logging camp, where he worked and slept rolled in the coverlet." The woolen yarn was not originally spun for the coverlet. It had already walked miles on many feet in the form of long knitted socks. When the socks began to have holes, they were set aside as "footlins" to be unraveled and dyed. These footlins eventually were woven into a handsome warm coverlet by Dulcena for Miss Montgomery's grandfather.

There is documentation of Dulcena's marriage and tract of land where she and her husband farmed in Stark, County of Cook. The town record and family Bible date Dulcena's death on March 22, 1902 and give her age as eighty-three years, two months and twenty-three days.

Deeds and sale of land show that Dulcena and her husband owned a sixty-acre tract of land sold to Dulcena's brother-in-law, giving up Dulcena's dowry rights to it. However, Dulcena remained on the farm, perhaps in return for helping her brother-in-law in some way. The small baby's blanket woven for Miss Montgomery's brother Oscar, who was born April 22, 1893, would mean that Dulcena Dewey, in her sparse and rugged way of life, had continued to spin, weave, and dye late into the nineteenth century. Her heart was full of spirit and color. The boy's blanket, now in the author's possession, is woven of fine white linen warp, with alternating one-fourth-inch stripes of single-spun natural sheep's gray, orange, and reddish orange, an unusually bright and handsome blanket for a baby.

References to the traveling tailor are further evidence of the fact that much cloth was made at home, but set aside until someone professionally trained could make it up into clothing. The tailor was described in *The Yankee Peddlars of Early America* by J. R. Dolan. He writes that the professional tailor would travel from house to house. The fabric he cut, sewed, and fitted was spun, dyed, and woven by the women of the household. The mistress of the house would feed and house the tailor while he worked at fashioning a suit for her husband that she was not skilled enough to fit. Such homespun suits would last for years.

Alice Morse Earle also writes of the traveling tailor and the many persons involved in the processes of the cloth before the tailor saw it. In the book *In Old Narragansett*, published in 1898, she quotes a Miss Hazard's words in telling of the production of cloth in her great-grandfather's home "from the shepherd who dogged the sheep, the wool-comber who combed the wool, the spinners who spun, the weavers who wove, all in regular order till the traveling tailor made the clothes up, and Thomas Hazard went to meeting in a suit made from wool of his own growing."

VILLAGE OR PUBLIC WEAVERS

Although many farmwives continued for generations to do most of their household weaving, for those who could afford it, usually by bartering, the village weaver, or "public weaver," was a welcomed addition to the rural communities from early times. While a number of professional weavers are known to have set up thriving shops in Boston and other seaport towns, the village weaver usually worked out of his loft room or shop in his home. He, too, farmed his land but augmented his living on a semiprofessional basis as a weaver for the townspeople. This skilled artisan was usually a male member of a family of professional weavers abroad. By settling in a New England town, he established his trade as a family enterprise, often handed down father to son. Some records indicate that village weaving flourished for several generations in one family. The weaver and his sons could weave large quantities and varieties of textile designs for the women in the villages, who often brought him their own homespun yarns to use.

Sometimes the village weaver was a man of multiple specialties. One such enterprising man was a carpenter and weaver of Suffield, Connecticut. His account book is, like many others, a revelation as to the variety of his days and skills. The following excerpt is taken from John Fitch Parson's account book, as it appeared in Charles Bissell's *Antique Furniture in Suffield, Connecticut, 1670–1835.*

Sept. 1804   Gad Taylor
honing 2 rasors, set of waggin boxes, a burow [bureau], a dining table, weaving 13 yards of cloath.
Frederick Taylor—
1809—a clockcase, a fireboard, weaving 16 yards cloath, putting a handle on a chopping nife.
John Dewey—1809—beaurow & dining table delivered to John Luis, a sideboard, a jointer [stool], a clockcase delivered to Doct Peas, a shuttle, tool shad, my waggin to hampton, a press bedstid for Shadrick Trumble, a pare of tables, a bedstid common, flackseed [flaxseed]
Samuel King—1809—a field bedstid, a one horse waggin, my waggin to Westfield, preparing a table, a small coffin, 2 bedstids

Frances Little refers to an earlier account book of a professional weaver who worked in the Salem, Massachusetts area that listed the labor connected with preparations of yarns and materials woven. In the account books of the weaver, named Hovey, this was itemized for one customer: "bag cloth, chekerd aprons, coverlid, druget, fine wool, linen cloth, sheting cloth, striped cotton, + 16 yd of napkins, boielin out the yarn, warping, spreding your flex, + combing yarn." Judging from the list of items he was an eighteenth-century weaver.

Abbott Lowell Cummings's article "Connecticut Homespun" (see Bibliography) relates that a family in Stonington, Connecticut carried on the trades of farming, running a sawmill, weaving, and dyeing. Josiah Newell was born in 1722 in the home his father settled in. He later raised a new home there in 1768 after his father's death. There he and his son Amos carried on the farming and weaving business. Account books begin in 1791 and continue until a year before Amos's death in 1844. Listed frequently are twenty- or thirty-yard orders of "cloth" and "linen cloth"; also itemized are "10 yds of bedtick," "shirting," and "flannel." Neighbors are credited in the accounts with having helped in the preparation of flax raised on the farm by breaking and spinning flax. Dyeing also was done by the family with a recipe book listing colors such as "chocolate," "clarret," "olive green," "snuf," and "scarlet." All were produced by careful measured amounts of dyestuffs and mordants, e.g., "to darken it take 4 pounds of log wood to thirty yard of cloth." Typical directions called for lots of "boyling" and then instructed the reader to "fling away your old dy and rence your cloth clean."

Amos's oldest daughter, Olive Newell, continued in the weaving tradition when she married in 1811, as did most women in Stonington, despite the availability of manufactured textiles. She saw to raising and producing both food and cloth for her family well into the nineteenth century. Even after cotton was available in the 1820s and flax was no longer raised, the family kept some thirty sheep for winter woolen underclothes, the wool spun by her daughters and woven by Olive Newell Walkley.

Some professional weavers were merchant tailors much in demand who made their livings in villages.

Nina Fletcher Little states that Tristram Coffin, Jr. carried on the business of merchant tailor in his house in Newbury, Massachusetts. He was the son of Tristram Coffin, the founder of a famous branch of the Coffin family in Nantucket. Tristram, Jr. lived in the original homestead his father had settled in 1642 in Newbury. Tristram, Jr. and his wife Judith married in 1693 and later had eleven children, all raised in the house. One of his sons, Nathaniel, worked with him in the business, for it required much spinning and weaving. They custom wove forty-five-inch width materials of cotton and wool in large quantities. Their record book or "day book" in the house has lists of names still familiar to the region, the descendants of the customers—Titcombs, Baileys, Noyeses, Doles—living there today. Nathaniel grew to manhood and was a member of the town selectmen and was town clerk. His son, in turn, was selectman and town clerk. Seven successive generations of Coffins lived in the house. It stands today on High Road in Newbury. An interesting architectural feature in the sitting room is a window, small and glazed, cut in the wall; traditionally, this was so that the lady of the household could see into the kitchen to overlook the spinners.

Alice Morse Earle's accounts of weavers in her book *In Old Narragansett* are fascinating and amusing. She writes that handweaving was a very respectable occupation for men as well as women and that the province was full of weavers. The spinning jennies supplied the yarns, but there were no industrial power looms until 1812. According to the author, "the prince of Narragansett weavers was Martin Read," who was baptized in St. Paul's church in 1761. He was then an adult and the parish clerk, and sexton for many years. "He led the singing, and it is said that under his leadership the Venite was first chanted in America." During the Revolution he helped read morning prayers and services for the dead. His career was interesting. As an orphan he was apprenticed to a linen weaver at the age of seven. He served as apprentice until he came of age; then he learned more about weaving. "He married the daughter of an Irish weaver, and soon had journeymen and apprentices, whom he taught to sing as they wove; and . . . with singing and whistling the work speeded." Singing and whistling have much in common with weaving, for as music has beats and rhythm, so has weaving the rhythm of the beater and the timing of the shuttle throw. These kept regular and even with the lilt of a song. Weavers had for generations accompanied their repetitious work to tunes with the right rhythm. Some sang psalms.

Martin Read "wove coverlets, blankets, broadcloth, flannel, worsted, linen, tow-cloth, and calmanco . . . also duroy, durant, and crocus."

Not far along the road from where Martin Read lived there worked a weaver christened William Henry Harrison Rose, but known as "Weaver Rose." He is perhaps the most intriguing of the weavers because we know more about him. He was the last of the village weavers who earned his living by handweaving. Not only was his work prolific, but his productivity continued well into the nineteenth century until he died in 1913 at age seventy-three. His work itself would be sufficient cause to be of interest, but as a human being he was rather special. To villagers who did not know him, walking by to fetch food or supplies, he was simply a rosy-cheeked, bearded, long-haired barefoot oddity. Little did they know of the spirit and discipline of his mind. In reading accounts of his life, and hearing remembrances of persons living today who knew him, we find much more. He was not only a highly productive and creative weaver, but a well-read scholar, primarily self-taught. He was considered an authority on classic literature, and a naturalist. He loved animals, and owned a few cows, a horse, and four dogs.

Weaver Rose was proud of his heritage and was a true American in every sense. Alice Morse Earle writes in 1898 of his colorful patriotic lineage: "Weaver Rose would be an unimpeachable candidate for many of our modern patriotic hereditary societies. One great-great-grandfather held a commission under King George III. Others were members of provincial assemblies. Two great-uncles were taken on board a Yankee privater in the Revolution. . . . The son of one . . . was captured in the War of 1812, and kept eight years at Dartmoor. . . . [When released, he] held to his death an office under the government of Wickford, a Narragansett seaport. One great-uncle was starved to death in the prison ship Jersey in the Revolution, and another lost his life in Newport during imprisonment by the British. Grandfather James Rose was with the famous Kingston Reds in the battle of Rhode Island and other Revolutionary encounters; and the weaver's father, William Rose, fought in the War of 1812. His great-great-grandfather Eldred killed the famous Indian warrior, Hunewell, after that cruel Narragansett tragedy, the swamp fight. . . . This [occurred] about 2 miles from the weaver's home." Mrs. Earle continues about Rose's heritage. "Some of his ancestors were those who made the original Petaquamscut purchase from the Indians, and here he lives on the very land they purchased."

Weaver Rose, also known by the names of "Billy Rose" and "Quaker Billy," lived in a small house on Slocum Road in Kingston with his sister, Elsie, who also wove. Their house was a one-and-a-half-story Cape Cod cottage with an ell. Upstairs in the lofts over the house and ell he had his three looms, a myriad assortment of weaving equipment, including seventy to eighty reeds, and piles of yarn. His looms were built by local carpenters and were constructed, in the tradition of the eighteenth century, of heavy barn-frame pegged beams. One loom, on which he wove couch covers and portieres, was larger, being sixty inches wide. He used drafts handed down from Martin Read, whose apprentice had taught Rose when he was young, and drafts of his mother and grandfather, which apparently were numerous at one time. His mother's family had been weavers also. Weaver Rose wrote to Mrs. Earle that his grandfather "owned a shore [in Rhode Island] and fished in the spring and wove some at home and went out amongst the larger farms working at his trade of weaving whilst his wife carried on the weaving at home and had a number of apprentices." He continued with regard to his own trade, "More money can be made by weaving than by farming. I have woven 30 yards of rag carpet in one day at 10 cents a yard [ca. 1898] or 23 cents if I found the warp." Weaver Rose also managed his own farm, but spent most of his time weaving. His production of coverlets was prolific. Dr. George E. Pariseau of Maryland was known to have collected over 300 of his coverlet drafts written on brown paper, cardboard, backs of advertisements, and even on pine boards. Quite a number of his coverlet patterns gained fame and were widely known and appreciated. People from all walks of life would find his house and stop to place an order. His business card reveals he thought of himself as a "weaver of rag carpets, portieres, Hap-Harlots, and coverlets." He also was known for the many coverlet patterns he adapted for pillow tops and floor carpets. A variety of his work is today in the textile collection of the University of Rhode Island at Kingston, and is also to be found throughout the country, and at the White House and Smithsonian Institution in Washington, D.C.

The trade of the village and itinerant weavers was plied fairly constantly for many generations, as we see from the example of Weaver Rose's heritage and others. That the village weavers settled early in the colonies is confirmed by documentary evidence. The Massachusetts Historical Society has in its collections a contract dated 1640 for William Rix, weaver, for a small house. The contract is significant also in its perpetuation of a type of dwelling that weavers for generations in Europe and England had worked and lived in. It was a mere cottage of one room with a loft above. Often what seems to be new is actually an adaptation of a firm tradition. So it was in the life of the weavers such as Weaver Rose. They shared a traditional way of life that originated in England, Scotland, and Ireland.

A wool-weaver of the 1640s, with a piece of land to farm, cleared it, planted it, and gradually built his house—usually two stories high. In the upper story or loft he worked on his loom near windows. With money from his weaving he paid for his sheep, cow, or donkey, besides his rent and any extras. When his weaving was done, he took the material to the fulling mill, then home to check it well or burl and spread out to dry on frames. When it was dry, he took it to the weekly market and came home with money and more wool. His wife and children helped to card and spin the wool for him to weave again. The sound of the loom beating for this weaver of the seventeenth century was the same sound heard by Weaver Rose 200 years later.

Alice Morse Earle describes the weaver—a description fitting of today's weavers as well: "There was a monotonous yet well-controlled precision in this weaver's work that was most soothing. . . . This precision in work is that of the skilled hand and thinking brain controlling the machine. . . ."

THE ITINERANT WEAVERS

Instead of taking up a village residence, the itinerant weaver would travel with his loom knocked down, carried in his big wooden wagon. As the seasons would allow, he went from farm to farm, then on to the next township. He was often accomplished in seasonal farming chores as well as being an expert craftsman. He ate and slept with his temporary farm family, helping with preparing flax, farm chores, and odd jobs when his weaving duties allowed. Setting his loom up piece by piece in a room or a loft with a low bed provided (thus the hired man's bed), he worked through a season, then moved on to another farm where he was welcomed again. He must have been a curious part-time family member to those who were isolated in their small world on the farm, for he had been trained in Europe and traveled in and out of the hills of New England. His apprenticeship in the textile centers of England, Ireland, Scotland, or Europe meant he had become a highly trained professional. There he was taught the use of multiharnessed looms or draw-looms. His technical knowledge of complex and intricate patterns made his cloth the envy of the farmwife. Her four-harnessed loom could make beautiful geometrics large and small, but never had she seen handsome pictorial patterns such as the itinerant weaver showed her. The itinerant helped to make the pictorial coverlets far more popular in the rural communities than they were in the cities. Traveling with his loom to the remote areas of New England and eventually west, he wove names, dates, and patriotic symbols in the borders of choice patterned coverlets. These works of art and precision tell their own historic tales.

Sometimes the yarns were spun and dyed ahead by the women of the household in anticipation of an itinerant weaver's arrival. He and his book and samples of fancy patterns from which to choose were both a delight and timesaver. The farmwife did the choosing and he would do all the work of setting up and weaving.

Samuel Goodrich of Ridgefield, Connecticut, born in 1793, wrote in the 1820s memories of his childhood. The spinning of yarns and setting aside for the weaving to be done by an itinerant seemed common in the late eighteenth century. He wrote that each family made its own bread, soap, candles, butter, and cheese. "The fabrication of cloth, linen, and woolen was no less a domestic operation. . . . We raised our own flax, retted it, hackled it, dressed it and spun it. The little wheel [flax-spinning wheel], turned by the foot, had its place, and was as familiar as if it had been a member of the family. How often I have seen my mother and my grandmother, too, sit down to it—though this, as I remember, was for the purpose of spinning some finer kind of thread—the burden of the spinning being done by a neighbor of ours, Sally St. John. . . . The wool was also spun in the family, partly by my sisters, and partly by Molly Gregory, daughter of our neighbor, the town carpenter.

"The weaving of the cloth—linen, as well as woolen—was performed by an itinerant workman, who came to the house, put up his loom, and threw his shuttle, till the season's work was done."

Types of Looms

BARN-FRAME

The looms most frequently found and known to have been made and used in the seventeenth and eighteenth centuries were of barn-frame construction. The framework holding the working parts consisted of heavy hand-hewn beams, similar in appearance and thickness to those used for framing barns. They were fastened together at angles with large wooden pegs.

The large *back beam*, or *warp beam*, on which the unwoven *warp* (lengthwise yarn) was wound, was made of the trunk of a big tree. The *front beam* was the frame over which the woven material passed.

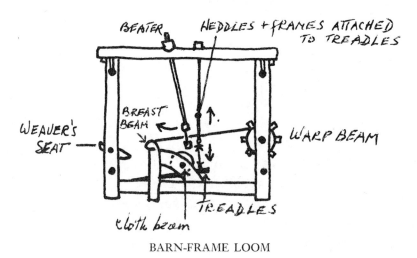

BARN-FRAME LOOM

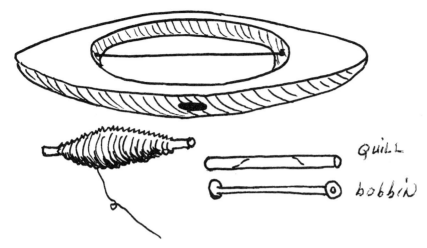

WOODEN BOAT SHUTTLE, PAPER QUILL, AND WOODEN BOBBIN

The shuttle has a wire spring for holding a bobbin or quill. The bobbin or quill was wound with yarn and its end drawn through the hole in the shuttle. The yarn unwound as the shuttle was thrown.

The warp yarns stretched between the front and the back beams were held under tension by a *dog* and *ratchet* while weaving took place. As the *web*, or woven material, progressed, it was wound onto a cloth beam. Releasing the tension of the dog and ratchet caused the warp yarn to move forward slightly a few inches; then the tension was tightened again, and weaving would progress for about two more inches. This procedure continued until the desired length of warp had been woven. Then it was cut from the loom or other items woven on the continuing warp yarn until the weaver had reached "the end of his rope." Whence comes the expression, for he could work the warp no more.

The actual weaving was accomplished by the moving parts of the loom. The *beater* hung by the overhead frame and swung freely from a position about one-third of the way from the front of the loom. The beater was pushed back out of the *shuttle*'s way with one hand as the latter passed from one side of the warp to the other. The weaver's hands changed beater for shuttle, shuttle for beater. As the shuttle passed back and forth the *weft*, formerly called *woof*, or crosswise yarn, unwound from the shuttle *bobbin*, or *quill*, and was beaten against the previously woven web with each synchronized swing of the beater. Set firmly

57

within the beater was the *reed*, or *slay*, as it was called in the seventeenth century. The reed consisted of narrow strips of marsh reeds set vertically into the horizontal reed frame at precisely regular spacing the full width of the beater. Thus the beater not only pressed the weft yarn against the web, but served as a means of setting and keeping the degree of closeness of the warp yarns consistent throughout the weaving. The vertical spaces on the reed were called *dents* or *splits*. Many reeds were needed by a weaver. These he changed and fastened firmly in the beater, according to the type of material he was going to weave. Reeds with many spaces per inch, say forty, would be called forty-dent reeds. Those with wide spacing, or setts, ten or twelve dents per inch, were used for rugs or coarse wools; while the finer-set reeds were used for finest linens. Some linen counts or setts were as high as sixty and eighty.

Before any beating or shuttle-throwing could take place, the ends from the warp yarns that were already wound on the large back beam, were threaded into the *heddles* on the heddle frames called harnesses, supported midway between the front and back by the upper frame structure. Sometimes the harnesses were referred to as *leaves*, or *shafts*. This *threading*, or *drawing-in*, step was done each yarn separately, one by one, across the width of the warp with the aid of a *reed-hook*. This was

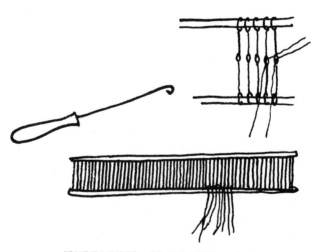

THREADING, OR DRAWING-IN

Each warp end was threaded, or drawn-in, by means of a reed-hook through the eye of the heddle. When all warp ends had been drawn-in, the reed-hook was used once again to pull them one by one through slits in the reed. This process was called slaying.

58

essentially a small handle with a flat hook on the end to grasp a thread and pull it through the eye or hole in the heddle. The harness frames, usually four, held a great many string heddles. The warp ends were drawn-in through the heddles in alternating harness frames according to a pattern followed precisely by the weaver. One thread out of place would be an error that would show up in the cloth as it was woven and run the length of the warp. When all the warp ends were through all the heddles, the next step was to use the reed-hook again and draw each warp end through the dents in the reed. This was called *slaying* from the old word *slay*, for dent. There were often literally hundreds of warp ends to draw-in and slay, all in their prescribed order. The harnesses were an important moving part in that they carried, by means of their many heddles, the warp yarns that were separated to allow the space, or *shed*, for the shuttle to fly across. The harness frames were attached by means of cords to the treadles at the base of the loom. This was called the *tie-up*. The weaver depressed a particular treadle or treadles with his feet, to pull down the harness to separate groups of warp threads while throwing the shuttle. These treadles were alternately depressed in a specific order to achieve a particular pattern. All of these procedures from the figuring and measuring of the warp length and the ends per inch, winding the warp, drawing-in the pattern, slaying the reed, tying-on to the cloth beam, to tying-up the treadles to the harness were not happenstance, but each carefully preplanned and predetermined to fulfill the end design and substance of the cloth itself.

Most looms, with the exception of the itinerants' multiharnessed looms, were basically of this two- or four-harness design. And the many steps required to *dress the loom*, or prepare it for weaving, were the same, regardless of the size, or whether it had two, four, five, six, or eight harnesses, or whether it was forty-five-inch, thirty-inch or twenty-seven-inch width. However, the smaller looms were not of such rugged construction. Some of the late nineteenth century were considerably lighter in construction and some were painted. One nineteenth-century loom, seen by the author in Marblehead, Massachusetts, was painted deep blue.

A great many coverlets, blankets, bed hangings, and sheets were woven on the forty-five-inch width looms. Table linens and toweling were traditionally woven by women for their dower. Possibly because of this tradition the smaller twenty-seven-inch looms were kept in use to a later period than the larger barn-frame loom. The farmwife's use of the barn-frame loom gradually gave way to the convenience of the village weaver and itinerants' big looms. However, many linens of twenty-seven-inch width were still woven in homes well into the late nineteenth century, indicating that women continued the tradition of weaving their own dower linens on the smaller-width looms.

Although English-made looms had been imported for home use, New England-made looms were manufactured about 1800. These were sold by peddlers for one-fourth the price of the English and were soon very popular.

TAPE LOOMS

Tape looms fell into a separate category of looms. They were plentiful and in all households. The wealthy had fancy tape looms in the parlor; others found them a dire necessity, as tape was used for many purposes. Narrow tapes were used for fastenings on clothing, ties on bonnets, pillow casings, tickings, loops on towels and curtains, drawstrings on bags and pockets, binding on bed hangings—for anything of fabric that needed tying, fastening, pulling, or hanging. Many tape looms were recorded in inventories.

The tape loom was a small upright rectangular board. The board was pierced with long narrow vertical slots, alternated with holes midway. Instead of harnesses with heddles to carry the warp yarns, the tape loom had built-in separators by way of the slots and the holes. The warp yarns were threaded into the alternating slots and holes; thus, the odd number of warp ends were in the long slots, and the even number in the holes. The odd number threads were raised with the hand, and the weft yarn was passed through the resulting opening (shed) and pressed down firmly, forming the web. The next shed was created by depressing the odd number in the slots lower than the yarns in the holes, thus raising them and forming an alternate opening. Usually the warp yarn was wound onto a small beam held in place. The long ends were tied to a chair or post. Warp yarn was either cotton or linen and weft yarn heavier linen or wool. Tapes for binding came in widths of ¼ inch, ⅜ inch, and ½ inch.

THE JACQUARD POWER LOOM

The Jacquard power loom, arriving in this country around 1830, had its influence in the cities, and wherever the professionally trained weaver, who was knowledgeable about the Jacquard weaves, located in the towns and villages of New England. He was now capable, with the Jacquard technique and other loom "mountings," of weaving pictorial designs on his multiharness fly-shuttle loom such as had never before been seen.

Warping Equipment

CLOCK-REEL

The clock-reel for winding skeins was a manually turned wheel on a base with a clock or dial that clicked when the required number of revolutions was wound; the skein was then tied. (See section on wool in chapter 2.)

SQUIRREL-CAGED REEL

This reel was used for stretching kinks in a skein of newly spun yarn. It was not used for measuring, as is erroneously thought.

SWIFT

The swift was an expandable rotating wooden device which held a skein for winding bobbins.

RADDLES

Raddles were rakelike spreading devices placed on loom temporarily while warping to keep segments of warp separated and evenly spaced as moving yarn was rolled onto warp beam.

NIDDY-NODDY

The niddy-noddy was an angled stretcher of wood predating the clock-reel as a primitive device for measuring skeins.

SPOOLS

Large wooden spools were used for winding the warp onto the warp beam. Many spools were set on a spool rack and then the ends were wound onto the warp beam.

WARPING FRAME

This was a square wooden frame with pegs a measured distance apart on which warp yarn was wound before proceeding to the warp beam on the loom. Those frames surviving have pegs for as much as 20–30 yards, substantiating that warping was put on the loom for several projects at one time.

The Weavers' Drafts

Alice Morse Earle wrote of Weaver Rose, "He has a worn pattern book of bewildering rules for setting the heddles for over fifty designs." In this she was referring to the *threading drafts* for drawing-in the pattern. A weaver's draft could also include the *treadling* (foot) directions, and all other necessary information, such as the size of the warp and weft yarns, how to slay the warp yarns or set them in the reed, and the size of the reed and how many dents it should have. To one nineteenth-century weaver treadling was known as the "Treaden Draft" and the threading on the heddles in harnesses as the "Harnish Draft." He might also write his own notations, such as this quote from an early nineteenth-century weaver's draft: "These is a good cord twell [twill] to the right hand [diagonal line from left to right] 1620 warp [ends]

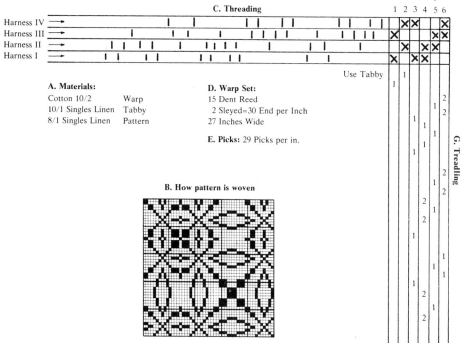

F. Tie-Up

C. Threading

| | 1 2 3 4 5 6 |

Harness IV
Harness III
Harness II
Harness I

Use Tabby

A. Materials:

Cotton 10/2 — Warp
10/1 Singles Linen — Tabby
8/1 Singles Linen — Pattern

D. Warp Set:

15 Dent Reed
2 Sleyed=30 End per Inch
27 Inches Wide

E. Picks: 29 Picks per in.

G. Treadling

B. How pattern is woven

ADAPTATION OF MURPHY'S "FOUR-LEAFED TWEEL" OR FOUR-HARNESSED TWILL IN PATTERN: A COARSER DIAPER OR LINEN WEAVE

A. *A medium fine weight two-ply yarn (i.e., one with two threads twisted together), is dressed onto the loom and serves as the warp yarn. It is purchased as size 10/2. The 10/1 singles linen is a medium fine weight single-ply yarn. The pattern yarn (or dark area of pattern diagram) is of heavier weight single-ply linen.*

B. *Each dark block in the pattern diagram represents floating pattern thread, or overshot thread, that covers the warp threads; i.e., three blocks of darkened squares means that three warp threads are covered by the pattern thread. The background (or white area of diagram) is made by weaving alternate throws of tabby (plain) weave with alternate throws of pattern (dark) yarn. The background (white) yarn always weaves the plain weave, whereas the pattern shuttle reflects the changes in the treadling as it is alternated with the background shuttle. Thus the background yarn binds in the changing pattern yarn.*

C. *Each mark in a harness space represents one warp thread drawn through the eye of one heddle on one harness frame. As the pattern of marks alternates, so the warp yarn is threaded consecutively, following the pattern.*

D. *Warp set means how close the warp yarns are placed together in the reed. Two ends are slayed into each slit, or dent, of the 15-dent reed. This makes 30 warp ends per each inch of warp width. Since the warp is 27 inches wide, there are 810 warp ends across width of warp.*

E. *Twenty-nine picks per inch means that in order to produce a good firm weave the weft thread (thrown by shuttle) should be thrown 29 times for 29 threads per woven inch. The finished towel should be woven to a length of 60 inches.*

F. *The boxes below Tie-Up represent the treadles, 1 to 6. They are fastened to the harnesses by cords in the manner prescribed by the Xs.*

G. *Treadling consists of depressing a treadle by foot. The treadle, in turn, pulls down the harnesses carrying the set of threads as set into the threading pattern (C). This creates the separation of warp yarns, allowing the shuttle to pass through in front of the weaver. Treadling is read from top to bottom, always alternating tabby throws with pattern throws in treadling sequence. The numerals in the columns for treadles 1 and 2 represent tabby throws, while the numerals in the columns for treadles 3 through 6 represent pattern throws. Begin at the top of the column for treadle 6. The 2 at the top of this column means that treadle 6 should be depressed twice, but a tabby throw must intervene between each depression of the treadle. Carry out the instructions as follows: Depress treadle 6, then treadle 2, then treadle 6 again, then treadle 1. Now move on to treadle 5, depress it once, and proceed in a similar manner.*

16 yarn [to the inch] 2 threads in the split [2 warp ends in each reed split, or dent] for wooll filling [use a wool weft]."

The threading drafts look like curious music on a five-line staff. The spaces represent the harness frames or shafts holding the heddles, and the marks in the spaces where notes would be, if the draft were a sheet of music, represent one thread in one heddle on one of the harnesses, counted one to four, front to back. Weaver Rose explained threading, or drawing-in, in a letter to a friend: "will try to [explain] how to begin to draw [,] draw one thread on the First Shaft then one on the second Shaft that makes 2 then one on the First Shaft makes 3 one on the second that is 4."

The weaver's draft also shows the tie-up, or how the treadles should be connected to the harness frames, so that when the proper treadle is depressed the desired combination of harnesses go up and down. The threading in the heddles is designed to make groups of threads rise and fall. This creates the pattern as the weft yarn is thrown back and forth in the opening shed. Sometimes the treadles can be tied-up to different harnesses, thus creating a different pattern from the same threading. The letters WADI on a draft stand for "woven as drawn in," meaning that the tie-up was a standard one and that the treadling was to follow consecutively the way the pattern was threaded onto the harnesses. One early draft simply stated it "Tromp as writ," which would give many a weaver a chuckle.

Rhythm was an important part of producing a good evenly woven cloth. The methodical swing of the beater, along with a steady throw of the shuttle and accurate, deft treadling of the feet, were components of the whole rhythm. One weaver indicated in his draft the importance of the rhythm of the footwork. Murphy says of a particular "Tweel" a certain even number of treadles were advised "to make the treading of the feet alternate without interruption."

The illustration on page 63 shows a weaver's draft. It explains an old weaver's pattern dated 1827 and used prior to that date, and contains an adaptation for a four-harness counterbalanced loom of today.

The Godbertson inventory of 1633, as reconstructed with items similar to those in the original. Note the high ratio of bed furnishings and linens to furniture, tools, and utensils. In the foreground are sheeting, blankets, two bed rugs, tablecloths, a piece of Irish linen, a curtain, pillows and pillow cases, bolster and featherbed, and two deerskins. Furniture consisted of basics: a chair, table, and two chests and boxes. Tools for hunting, farming, carpentry, and kitchen use are the remaining items, along with clothing. Godbert Godbertson and his wife Zarah died the same year in Plymouth, Massachusetts, without heirs. Their inventory is considered of value for insight into one household's total necessities at that time.—Photograph courtesy Plimouth Plantation

Stone cottage keeping room. The cottage was built in 1840 as a farmer's tenant house in South Burlington, Vermont. It has three rooms, including the keeping room, downstairs and a children's room in the garret upstairs.

A red and white plaid woolen blanket is hung from a crane as a shield from drafts. Overhead two handwoven blankets, one in blue and white checks and one with windowpane crosslines, are kept in storage on suspended rods. All the blankets are woven in twill with single-ply woolen yarn. At the window is a loop-hung curtain of linen, and a hooked rug is at the hearth. The unique oak chair is probably of Canadian origin.—Photograph by John M. Miller courtesy Shelburne Museum

Northwest bed chamber in the Dutton house (circa 1782), Shelburne, Vermont. The tester bed, painted an orange red, dates from the late eighteenth or early nineteenth century, and has all-white furnishings of the early to midnineteenth century, including spread and lace-trimmed flounce, along with fringed valance and loop-top bed curtains of dimity. The white candlewick spread is handwoven of three strips each thirty inches wide. Woven of a crossbar design, the candlewicking is in the tree of life and floral pattern. Notice the matching trimmed dimity window curtains. On the floor is a handloomed cotton rag rug in variegated colors.—Photograph by John M. Miller courtesy Shelburne Museum

*Northeast bed chamber in the Dutton house (circa 1782). The low
bed with double-arched headboard is covered with a handwoven
wool counterpane. Sewn up the center, the two pieces have the name
of the maker, Phebe Rice, cross-stitched. She embroidered crescent-
or lunette-shaped motifs around three sides (seven in blue, sixteen in
two shades of ginger and tan). Flowers and leaves have been
embroidered at the point of the crescent, and the bottom of the
counterpane has been rounded off. A thick fringe of blue wool is
around three sides of the counterpane. Floor rug is warp-striped
carpet with rag filler, seamed in panels.*—Photograph by John M.
Miller courtesy Shelburne Museum

chapter 3

TABLE LINENS

*T*HE USE OF tablecloths and napkins from the seventeenth century on is evident by the large quantities listed and the frequency with which they appear in even modest household inventories. The wealthy listed "duzzens" of napkins, the not-so-wealthy listed comparatively large numbers. Table linens are repeatedly listed throughout the 1630s into the nineteenth century and were in daily use.

As early as 1633, Samuel Fuller Thelder of Plimouth, Massachusetts listed among other items, "15 table napkins, 3 tablecloathes . . . 8 table napkins." The value of table linens, as well as bed linens, surprisingly exceeded that of other furnishings we today would assume more costly. The Godbertson husband-wife inventory of the same year in Plimouth listed among their meager possessions "a tableclouth" whose value was equal to the combined value of "a chaire" and "a chest." Henry Harwood of Salem, Massachusetts in the year 1664 listed his "3 p. of sheetes, 1 duzzen of napkins" at the value of one-seventh his total household furnishings.

The concept of dining in the seventeenth century seems unusual to us now. The food was prepared in the keeping room and eaten there on the great board or trestle table, made of plain boards placed on trestles.

In 1678 at Portsmouth, New Hampshire, Richard Cummings declared in his will, "Furthermore, I give to yᵉ sᵈ Richᵈ [the said Richard] Joye yᵉ best bed in yᵉ House with all yᵉ Furniture thereto belonging, with yᵉ *Tableboard* & *Joyn-stooles* [joined stools] in yᵉ new house. . . ." A tablecloth used on the "long table board" was called a "borde cloth," the earliest name for tablecloth. Mr. Wilton Gilson of Scituate in 1639 listed a relatively high value of twelve shillings for his "table linen napkins & boardcloths." Sometimes the dining took place in the great hall or parlor, near a warming fire, not far from the great bed. The food was either brought to the great hall from the keeping room after being prepared, or it was cooked at the fireplace in the great hall. It was commonly acceptable to dine with guests there. The round or smaller-framed table was usually covered with a thick imported carpet used for this purpose, as carpets were not walked upon at that time. They were either hung on walls as tapestries were, or thrown over tables, sometimes reaching to the floor. The table carpet was covered with a linen tablecloth for dining purposes. Bearing in mind that forks were not commonly used until well into the eighteenth century, it is easy to imagine eating and cutting as messy procedures. The knife was the main tool for eating, together with some spoons. The meat was placed on a *common server*, or *charger*, and each person used his knife, if indeed he had one of his own, to carve off a portion, holding the meat with his other hand in order to cut. It is assumed other foods, such as shellfish, were eaten with the fingers. Liquids and broths from a shared bowl or tankard went directly to the mouth. Trenchers and plates were shared also. It is not hard to understand that napkins served an important use for wiping the fingers and hands, and protecting seldom cleaned clothing.

Early napkins, according to European paintings of the period, were large rectangles, sometimes oblong, covering the lap and knee. Table-cloths are also depicted placed over the table carpet. Some tablecloths mentioned in inventories are described as being from three to five yards long. Several shown in Flemish paintings appear to be square, some round.

Another piece of linen mentioned in seventeenth-century inventories, but not as frequently, is the *cupboard cloth*. This was possibly used on finer cupboards such as a court cupboard. Large pewter or imported china bowls may have been placed on it for display, as such cupboards were enclosed, more like ornate chests. Some cupboard cloths hung as much as halfway down the side of the cupboard.

Among linens of interest that William Kempe of Duxborrow (Duxbury) itemizes in his will of 1641 is a "wrought [embroidered] cupboard cloth." For the parlor he lists the following items: "5 paire of flaxen sheets, 1 paire of new hampen, 2 duzzen of fine napkins and 2 tablecloathes, 1 sheete, 5 Holland pillow coats [cases], 2 duzzen of course napkins, 3 pair of old pillow coats, 7 course towells, 3 course tablecloathes, 1 hand towell, 1 remnant of Holland, 2 short table cloathes, 2 yards of white fusteon [fustian], 1 wrought Holland cubberd cloth, 3 smale pillowes, 1 spinning wheel."

Seaborn Cotton of Hampton, New Hampshire lists in his will of 1684, along with bed furnishings, "Red coverlid, carpett, and cupboard cloths, but if my son John dye without lawful issue, I will them all, if *not worne out* . . . to the next heire male, borne among my daughters." He also writes, "Besides . . . I give to Elizabeth, a table cloath and six nap kins, marked R. O. said to bee given her by Mʳ. Richard Oliver, at my decease, or her marriage."

As frequently as table linens do appear in the early listings, it would seem unlikely that the first table linens were home-woven in the colonies. Rather, they were brought with other household items and clothing from Europe or England. Communication with England was not a problem for the first twenty years, as ships arrived frequently, bringing new immigrants with their belongings and more provisions. Nevertheless, these early imported linens were part of established and continuing traditions that people in rural areas clung to. There is evidence of early looms, weaving gear, and items such as "1 piece of loomework" in Massachusetts as early as 1633, but the looms at first were few and probably used for the fundamental need of keeping the colonists warm, i.e., weaving blankets and clothing. Inventories include table linens such as diaper (dieper, diap^r), Holland, and Dowlas. Although these were originally imported, home weaving of linens did begin after the first two decades or so. Therefore, the types of weaves warrant description.

Table Linen Weaves

DIAPER

Diaper, or dieper, had its beginnings in the form of a silk fabric with a tiny diamond or square pattern, and was woven in Ypres, Belgium. The Greek word *diaspron* means "small-figured." The diaper pattern of linen received its name as a contraction of *cloth d'Ypres* and *diaspron* into the English word "diaper." The small geometric figures were used in the manufacture of linens in Holland and eventually England, Scotland, and Ireland, as the production of flax increased in these countries. In the seventeenth century, the pattern was extremely fine-woven in all-white linen, and was primarily used for napkins, tablecloths, towels, board cloths, and cupboard cloths. It gradually changed to a somewhat less than fine fabric and at a later period is described by the professional weaver, John Murphy, in his book, *A Treatise on the Art of Weaving*, 1827: "The finer kinds, which usually are woven by a more extensive apparatus [than dornic], and, in general, with a tweel [twill] and five leaves [harnesses] are called diaper."

HOLLAND

Holland was a very fine plain linen weave of superior quality. It was originally imported from Holland and was used for tablecloths and napkins.

DORNIC

Dornic, also known as dornoc and dornick, was also described in

John Murphy's book on weaving mentioned above and included with diaper, as having been manufactured in Dornock, in the north of Scotland. He infers that dornic linens, woven with less counts or threads per inch "having only a four-leafed tweel were manufactured in considerable quantities. . . ."

HUCK

The words "huck" and "hucka-back" are of German origin, from "hukkeback," meaning peddler's wares. Huck is a strong cloth woven of grouped threads making cords or ribs in the cloth, also sometimes giving the appearance of small blocks of floating threads. The grouped

Table linens. On left: *bird's-eye diamond linen weave with two-ply cotton fringe applied, 52 inches square, excluding fringe, seamed down center.* On right: *all-linen, single-ply woven in M's and O's plaid, 29-inch panel seamed in center, 58 by 61 inches. Both items woven by Olive Sargent of Brattleboro, Vermont.*—Old Sturbridge Village photograph by Donald F. Eaton

73

cords alternate as weft yarns are woven across. This weave was used for toweling, tablecloths, and napkins.

M's and O's, one of the enlarged forms of hucka-back, was also called "Buchens and Owls" and termed as a diaper weave. It was used for tablecloths, napkins, and toweling in many variations of blocks and plaids. It was made in linen up until the early nineteenth century, when cotton M's and O's were considered much more up-to-date; by the mid-nineteenth century it was commonly used with tied fringe for tablecloths and napkins.

BIRD'S-EYE

This is a form of diaper which persisted into the nineteenth century in many variations—for instance, enlarged with concentric diamonds called triple-draught bird's-eye, and set in blocks with large diamonds. It was used for toweling and table linens.

DAMASK

This weave of all linen had an alternating spacing of satin and dull weave plaid achieved by alternating warp and weft-faced twill in pattern blocks. Only the simplest forms of damask were possible on the four-harness home looms, but these were strikingly handsome in their simplicity. Itinerant and professional weavers were capable of more intricate designs. Later diaper damasks were woven at home with linen warp and purchased cotton filler weft.

The patterned white linen tablecloth was a symbol of monetary success in the seventeenth and eighteenth centuries, and a great many were made by the housewife.

The tradition of women weaving their own toweling, bed linen, and table linens for their dowries was firmly established in the late seventeenth century, along with the immigration of the experienced Scottish and Irish linen weavers. Many of the linen patterns of white on white were handed down from mother to daughter for generations and used in table linen and toweling. Although many other items were eventually made by itinerants and mills, this tradition continued; the large barn-frame loom was eventually used less or forsaken, but the smaller twenty- to twenty-eight-inch looms were kept for the weaving of dowry linens into the nineteenth century.

From an early date looms, flax-raising, and woven table and bed linens were mentioned in inventories. New Hampshire and Massachusetts inventories have repeated accounts from the late seventeenth century on into the late eighteenth century. It is documented "that as early as 1677 John Paine of Salem had 'home made napkins'."

Frances Little in her *Early American Textiles* makes reference to Connecticut and Rhode Island inventories that also bear out the fact of home linen weaving and spinning. Some excerpts from these inventories follow.

1643—Thomas Scott, Hartford
2 tablecloths, 3 "dyeper" napkins
        5 flax napkins
5 pair sheets [3 flax, 2 tow]

1648—Timothy Standly
Hemp & flax, linen yarn, 2 linen wheels
1 wool wheel, [quantities of linen]

1635—Thomas Hooker
great amounts of household linen,
wheels as well

1716 Obadiah Brown, R. I.—
had flax, sheep, 2 linen wheels, dressed hemp,
linen cloth, dressed flax, a hatchel, & tow yarn.

1725—Arthur Fenner, R. I.
2 looms/harnesses, slays, warping bars
4 spinning wheels, worsted cards, clock-reel.

A matching towel was not uncommon along with napkins and tablecloth. Some early table linens were probably imported. These were available in various qualities of diaper weave, judged according to the fineness of the sett of threads. They are listed as fine, middling diaper, or coarser sett.

Dimensions of the earliest napkins can only be guessed, but were certainly large by our present-day standards. In 1688 two dozen napkins required an order of twenty-six yards of linen. This would allow more than one yard per napkin, along with hemming. Marion Day Iverson writes in her article "Table Linen in Colonial America" that the Metropolitan Museum of Art has a documented napkin from a Holland workshop. The damask is dated 1663 and measures 42 by 29½ inches. Napkins were much in use and a necessity, considering that fingers and knives were still the tools of eating in rural areas as late as 1754. Forks were available then but not commonly used. The use of the table napkin in the early, mid, and late seventeenth century seemed essential and is well substantiated by inventories. When the use of forks became common in the 1780s, the napkins were spared and the tablecloth instead was used. For guests the table was "covered," but guests as well as family wiped their fingers on the tablecloth. The cloth must have been a chore to wash and rather unsightly after the many courses typical of the times! Even wealthy homes made little use of napkins until the late eighteenth or early nineteenth century, when it was again considered proper to have neatly folded napkins at the table and a tablecloth as well.

A late eighteenth-century tablecloth in the Copp Family collection in the Smithsonian Institution is presumed home-woven in the diaper pattern of M's and O's. Woven in two 22-inch width panels, probably on a small loom, it has a 61-per-inch thread count. Measuring 45 by 57 inches, it has a woven 1⅛-inch fringe of cotton loop applied on all four sides, suggesting the fringe was added at a later date. Some indication of napkin shape becoming more square during the late eighteenth century is documented by matching M's and O's napkins measuring 21 inches by 22 inches.

Towel dimensions vary only slightly over a long period. Gallagher's *Linen Heirlooms* (see Bibliography) records many from different locales. One towel from Norwell, Massachusetts woven in basket weave with blocks of plain weave dated as early as 1767 measures 25½ inches wide by 36 inches long; one from Sandwich, New Hampshire woven in Bronson—a German "barleycorn weave" dated circa 1830—measures 20½ by 40 inches. A third, circa 1855, from Bridgton, Maine, woven in a diamond twill, measures 24¾ by 37 inches. All were woven on relatively small looms.

Handwoven utilitarian towels. On left: *dornick tow linen, showing a resemblance to over-shot coverlet patterns.* On right: *herringbone twill weave linen.* Underneath: *a dark tow with subtle twill and plain pattern. It is a fragment from Amherst, Massachusetts. The dornick patterned towel is woven of natural color tow in a bird's-eye diaper weave, the dornick being the coarser type of diaper weave. Its dimensions are 21 by 34 inches. It is hemmed by hand at both ends.*–Old Sturbridge Village photograph by Donald F. Eaton

It is noteworthy that the Whig Rose overshot pattern mentioned in *Linen Heirlooms,* traditionally thought to be a coverlet pattern, was one of many small overshot patterns that were first used for linens and later adapted with color wool for pattern yarn to the bed coverlet. In the linen tablecloth woven with the Whig Rose pattern the pattern and background tabby, or plain weave, are the same white linen. Tablecloths were woven on the smaller looms in two panels varying from 27 to 29 inches wide. One M's and O's tablecloth woven of linen circa 1757 in Salisbury, Massachusetts measures 56½ inches wide by 53 inches long, of two panels each 28½ inches wide. Tablecloth lengths vary, but the narrow 27- to 29-inch panels are relatively consistent.

Two linen tablecloths in the collections of the Essex Institute, Salem, Massachusetts, are in excellent condition and further attest to the traditional linen weaves that were found in New England. One tablecloth made of two 27½-inch panels, measuring 55 inches by 58 inches, was woven in single-ply linen, as most were, by Miriam M. Hastings, Lyman, New Hampshire. It is of particular interest in that the cloth's four-sided 1¼-inch fringe was not applied but woven and hemstitched as work progressed on the loom—a tidy trick, and beautifully worked. The linen pattern is a damask of alternating twill blocks and bird's-eye block. The other tablecloth was woven on a slightly larger loom, as were other items in the Essex collection by the same weaver, Mrs. Abram (Olive) Prescott. The pattern is a delicate miniature grouping of M's and O's widely spaced on a plain field. It was woven in 1840 in two panels of 34 inches and is 68 inches wide and 70½ inches long with a finely turned ⅛-inch hem. At the center of the tablecloth, written in a graceful script hand, is the identification, "Olive Prescott No. 5." Sheeting was often embroidered with initials and numbered. Olive apparently numbered her tablecloths also. She was the wife of Captain Prescott, who raised the flax and prepared it for her to spin and weave on their farm in Forge Village, Massachusetts, near the Groton line. She also wove a variety of traditional diaper-patterned towels in the collection.

Tablecloths were not always white. In the rural areas especially, from the mid-eighteenth to the early nineteenth century, they were listed as "strip'd [striped]," "plad," "cheks," "check'd," and "blew diaper."

Some were woven with China blue pattern linen on white, colored windowpane crosslines on white, and checks; some of the most handsome were traditional plaids. Most of these were woven in all linen, although nineteenth-century colored tablecloths sometimes had cotton warps with linen weft. Fine all-cotton tablecloths and napkins most often were factory produced, not handwoven.

In the Old Deerfield collection is a table linen in soft blue and white linen plaid of ⅜-inch size block. It was woven by Lucretia Hall of Charlemont (1750–1835).

Linens were also woven for kitchen purposes such as covering food. Cheeses and cakes were wrapped, crocks covered and tied, liquids strained with linen. An 1874 reference describes "Clouting Diaper" as "a quaint flower pattern on a spotted white ground" and speculates that the original use of linen so patterned may have been to strain clotted, or curdled, milk or cream for making cheese.

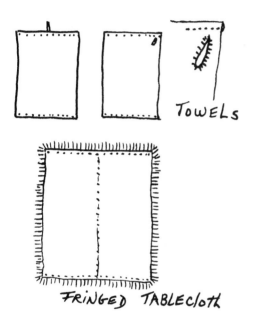

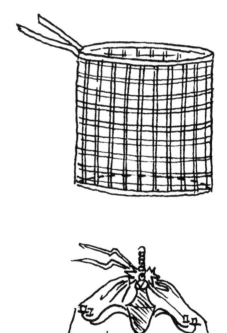

TOWELS AND TABLECLOTH

Utility and hand towels were hemmed with a ¼-inch turn. Tapes were sewn at the center top for hanging. Sometimes a buttonhole in the corner served as a hanging device. Tablecloths were seamed up the center. They usually had two panels, but sometimes had three. Fringe was applied on all sides of the tablecloth shown after its fine rolled hem was turned at top and bottom.

PLAID LINEN COVER FOR CHANDELIER

When warmer weather and longer daylight hours came, chandeliers were covered and not used. Protection was needed from flies and dust and dirt blowing in through windows. This cover is open at top and bottom with a narrow hem and casing for drawstring at top. Linen covers were also used to protect mirrors and paintings during warm weather.

79

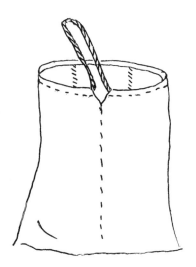

GRAIN OR FLOUR BAG

These bags, home-woven and -sewn, were made of three pieces for durability. Grain bags were made of coarsely spun and woven tow linen. Flour bags were closely woven of fine linen.

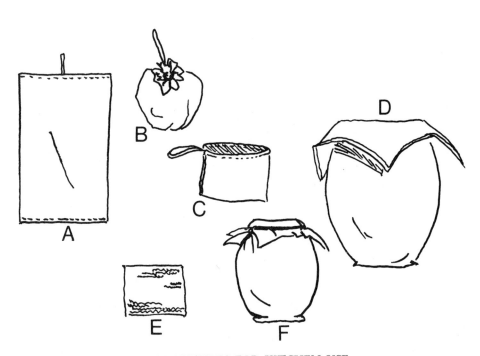

LINEN ARTICLES FOR KITCHEN USE

A. Utility towel. These towels of either coarse or fine linen were hemmed and sewn with tape loops for hanging. They were used to cover food, to dry dishes and hands, to wrap cheese during pressing and storage, and to wrap cake. Sometimes they were dipped in brandy to keep cake moist. Fine towels were used for straining liquids. B and C. Rag bags. Rough tow linen was made into rag bags with cords for drawing and hanging in the buttery. Two were always in use—one for clean rags, one for dirty. D. Piece of linen used to cover crock. E. Knitted washcloth of tow linen. F. Linen tied with string used to cover potted meat.

chapter 4

BEDDING

Bed Types

Among his household goods, the farmer prized his beds and their furnishings. The parents' bed, or *great bed*, was considered the most valuable bed in the house. It was a four-poster of approximately today's three-quarters size, with a straight tester frame from which a valance and bed curtains were hung. The foot posts of the seventeenth-century and very early eighteenth-century bed were usually covered with curtains and hence were made very plain. Later period beds from the mid-eighteenth century had end posts exposed, and these were more decorative. However, in rural areas the styles were late to change, and beds were simply made and lacking the elaborate post carvings of the wealthy.

81

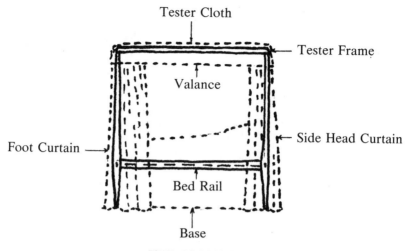

THE GREAT BED

Traditionally the great bed and its furnishings were willed to the eldest son. Sometimes the bed itself was handed down to the eldest son, while the bed curtains or bed hangings were divided among other sons and daughters, especially if the panels of the bed hangings had been embroidered, or "worked." A complete set from one bed, consisting of four or five panels, is seldom found today, since they were often dispersed into succeeding households of the several children. Museums and historical societies carefully preserve the few that still exist and only periodically display them.

Bed cords were the heavy twisted linen ropes, interlaced across bed rails from side to side and end to end as a foundation for the "bed-tick," or mattress and featherbed. The holes found in the foot and side rails of early beds were for lacing cords in and out and across. A *wrench*, sometimes mentioned with the cords, was used to tighten the cords as weather and wear might require.

It is not difficult to imagine how full of people a house might be in the eighteenth century. Aunts, uncles, grandparents, and cousins lived with the nuclear family as a normal way of life. But the farmwife often received added company to be bedded down for the night—hungry, weary travelers, relatives, and extra help when crops were to be harvested. Extra beds were needed for such emergencies. A new baby? The cradle was there by the great bed. More little cousins visiting? Two or

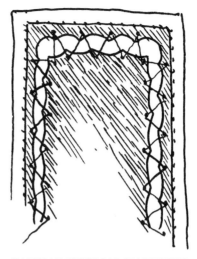

CANVAS-BOTTOM MATTRESS
This mattress, also called a sacking bottom, was sometimes used on a folding bed. When the canvas slackened, it could be tightened or laced by pulling the cords.

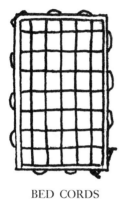

BED CORDS

three could sleep in the trundle bed, or underbed, pulled out from under the big bed. And there were more trundles under other beds in other rooms.

The four-poster great bed and the *half-headed folding bedstead* are perhaps the most interesting bed types of the seventeenth and eighteenth centuries. The folding bedstead, a functional extra, was far outvalued by the great bed as to monetary worth, but certainly must be acknowledged as the ingenious forerunner of the modern-day Murphy bed. Today it would be a handy guest bed for every home to have. But try to find one! Museums and collectors have most of them. They were commonly used throughout the eighteenth and into the nineteenth century, frequently in the kitchen or keeping room, as well as other rooms. The bed was hinged on the side rails about one-quarter to one-third of the distance from headboard to foot, sometimes having an extra set of legs at the hinge. When not in use, the foot end was raised to the wall, legs folded down, and curtains drawn together to conceal it neatly against the wall.

There was usually a *low bed*—a plain, narrow single bed in the

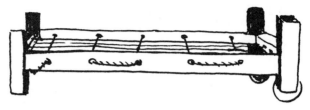

TRUNDLE BED

The bed has ropes to hold a straw mattress. Rollers on the foot end posts drew it out from under the large bed.

borning room off the keeping room—handy for sickness or a woman with a newborn baby. A low bed was also used in bed chambers throughout the house and in the kitchen. A *low post bed* was also made in wide widths and common in bed chambers, often sleeping three and four. It, too, accommodated trundle beds. Remember, our forefathers were of smaller stature and not accustomed to twentieth-century comforts.

The *hired man's bed* was a simple, narrow low bed, set aside in a lesser room where he stayed, though he ate and worked with the family while he helped with the crops and did chores to help the farmer.

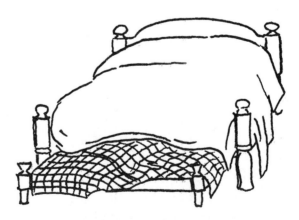

A TRUNDLE BED ARRANGEMENT

This wide low post bed, with trundle bed slightly pulled out, might sleep four to six people.

FOLDING BED

This bed usually had a hanging bed curtain and wall-hung valance. More rarely, it was stored in a press closet when not in use, or it may simply have been upended with no conceal-ment against the wall. The mattress may have been rolled with the bedding on and unrolled again when the bed was down, or it may have just oozed out around the edges.

SIMPLE LOW BED

The plain low headboard made this bed suitable for use under eaves. The bed shown has a bed-tick of checkered linen, stuffed with straw, woolen sheeting, and a blanket as coverlid.

Even the wooden high-backed fireside *settle* was used as a bed for an unexpected guest or traveler—a rather hard, inhospitable bed for a guest. Sitting bolt upright wrapped in wool blankets would seem a diffi-cult way to sleep, but perhaps a mug of hot rum and a blazing fire were compensation. A *bench bed* was a bench with seat that pulled down to open into a large boxlike bed that used a featherbed. Marion Day Iver-son writes in her book, *The American Chair, 1630–1890,* that a settle and two settle beds were owned by the elder William Brewster of Plym-outh before 1644. However, settle beds that have turned up in recent years in the northern United States are thought to be of Canadian origin.

85

West bed chamber of the Fenno house, the earliest house at Old Sturbridge Village, built in the late seventeenth century. On second floor, the low bed is covered with a home-woven overshot pattern coverlet. Carver-type chairs with rush seats have cushions attached by rear sewn loops. A simple blanket chest and folding gate table are also depicted. Wide floor boards are bare with exception of bearskin hide. Note lack of window curtains for this room. The coverlet dates from circa 1790–1810.—Old Sturbridge Village photograph by Donald F. Eaton

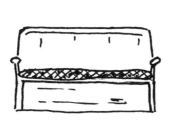 

BENCH BED

The lower part under the seat pulled down, providing a large drawerlike enclosure for bedding.

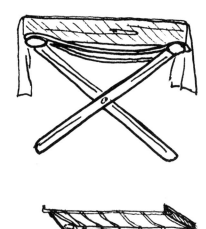

COT-TYPE BED

This bed had leather straps or rope joined by wooden pegs. Folded as a cot, it was moved from room to room. A corn husk or straw mattress was used on top of the straps.

The *field bed* was used during wartime in the field, and was folded to be carried for officers. It was similar in structure to the half-headed bedstead and could be folded to reasonably compact size. There was a rather unique *cradle bed* for the adult sick and elderly, shaped like a very large cradle with rockers. This bed could be tilted to make assisting a full-sized disabled person easier.

There were also cot-type beds with legs that folded and long side rails that held ticking in such a way as an army cot has stretched canvas. These cot-type beds, or *folding beds*, could be stored easily in a small space, and came in handy when many children overran the house.

The *undereaves bed* had low posts, no footboard and a low headboard. Sometimes it had shorter legs. It was popular from 1690 into the midnineteenth century because it utilized space. Later in the 1840s, when new machinery made possible new turnings, came the very popular *spool bed* or *Jenny Lind*. The legs, headboard, and footboard were made from lengths of uncut spool turnings and were usually painted. This bed was popular for many generations.

Although the pencil post bed was a popular type of country bed from 1750 on and was used in better country homes, most often the farmhouse had a variety of low beds, undereaves beds, a trundle bed or two, and half-headed folding bedsteads.

Regardless of the type of bed, the *bed furnishings*—the items of bedding that went into making the bed such as featherbeds, bolsters,

Lean-to room, second floor of Richardson house at Old Sturbridge Village, as it appeared in the late eighteenth and early nineteenth century. Low bed covered with home-woven checked indigo and white wool blanket, plain weave. Tucked in around cornhusk mattress over the ropes, the blanket completely covers bed. The pillow is set atop. The pillow's casing is a pieced combination of home-woven linen and blue plaid linen. A home-woven linen towel of diaper weave hangs on wash stand. On the peg is a work frock.—Old Sturbridge Village photograph by Donald F. Eaton

pillows, pillow casings, sheeting, blankets, coverlid, bed curtains, valances, and bases or flounces—were similar on all. In the will of John Hall of Greenland in the township of Dover, New Hampshire, drawn up in 1677, he states, "I give to my daught[R] Sara y[e] best Bed in ye porch-chamb wth y[e] Hangings & all Furniture, 2 p[R] of Sheets, Bolster, pillowes + y[e] 2 New Woollen Blankets—best Bedstead—Also I give to Abigail y[e] bed which is next to y[e] best with all Appurntenances suitable for it." Although we cannot be certain all of these items were hand-woven, it is possible at this time that some of them were. Nevertheless, these were the early traditional items that were the basic bed furnishings for almost two hundred years, with style changes mainly in what was termed the *bed furniture*, or outer dressings of the bed, including bed hangings, valances, testers, and coverlet.

Mattresses

FEATHERBED

The ingenious *featherbed* was designed for comfort as well as function. A known tradition in England and Europe as far back as the sixteenth and seventeenth centuries, it is now a long lost refinement. The featherbed of goosedown filling, covered in handwoven "bed tick," or ticking, was used in New England from the early seventeenth century far into the nineteenth century and remained the most preferred form of mattress even after other fillers had been made readily available. It continued to be highly valued into the nineteenth century. Today we have our light-as-air down comforts and the two-pound down-filled sleeping bag, but imagine the pounds and pounds of goosedown's soft caressing warmth on a blizzardy New England night! Blissful luxury! Goosedown today is still unsurpassed for warmth and comfort, although it is now used sparingly and is costly.

Featherbeds were frequently noted in inventories, always in the

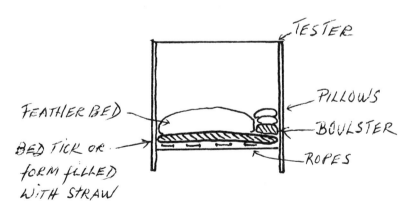

BASIC COMPONENTS OF THE GREAT BED

Filling materials were straw or corn husks for the bed-tick, straw or something equally firm for the bolster, and goosedown for both the pillow and featherbed.

context of bed furnishings belonging to the great bed or other beds. Sometimes itemized was a "bag of ffethers." When a goose was cooked, its plucked feathers were dropped into a bag and saved until there were enough for a featherbed or pillow. Feathers were also bought or traded. An interesting account was the will of a farmer in Portsmouth, New Hampshire in 1687. He wrote: "whereas Abigail Windiet my daughter which was not borne when my will was made I doe give unto her mother one bedticking which is in the house and one cowe to buy feathers to fill a bed & my daughter Abigail to have it when her Mother shall see it fitt with boulster to it."

FEATHERBED PLUMPER
This wooden paddlelike device was approximately two feet long.

FLOCK BED

The *flock bed* was also a mattress in common use in the seventeenth and early eighteenth century. It had been used in England as far back as the early fourteenth century. It was sometimes listed in inventories as a "flocke underbed," and perhaps was used under a featherbed or on a trundle bed. It was filled with coarse tufts or odd bits of wool, or even torn pieces of cloth, or sometimes wool combined with chicken feathers. "Flocke your mattress for wool is dere" was a common saying of the seventeenth century. In Act II of *Henry VII* (1495) reference was made to "Federbedds [featherbeds], bolsters and pillows made of . . . flokkis and feders togidre [flock and feathers together]." Sometimes the flock bed was the only mattress mentioned on a bed, usually a lesser bed such as a low bed. Or the flock bed was used on the floor over a pallet.

A flock bed is mentioned along with a feather bolster in the inventory of Will Wright, 1633, Plymouth, Massachusetts: "Oone little old fflock bed and an old fether bolster, wth a pre of worne sheets, an old greene rugge."

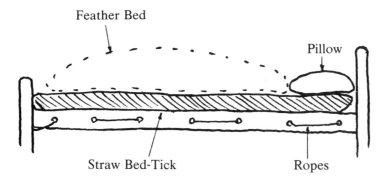

BASIC COMPONENTS OF THE LOW BED

The straw bed-tick to cover the ropes was the usual mattress. A featherbed and/or pillow were sometime luxuries.

BED-TICK

Bed-tick, or *bed-ticking*, was a general name for mattress. It could be confusing as these were also terms used for the covering itself. Bed-ticking was a finely woven striped or checked linen, or linen and wool. This was sewn into a large, enclosed pillowlike sack, and usually filled with straw, or in summer, corn husks, which were cooler to sleep on. There were other fillings as mentioned above. Although early bed-ticks were woven on a linen warp, in the late eighteenth and early nineteenth centuries, cotton was available from cotton mills for warp. The weft continued to be homespun linen.

OTHER MATTRESSES

There were other kinds of lesser mattresses with an odd assortment of stuffings, including a *chaff bed*, filled with the chaff from wheat and other grains, and a *cattail bed*, undoubtedly stuffed with the outer fibrous part of the cattail removed from the harder core and stem. Straw was a commonly used filler for a *straw bed*. Not so common and rather curious was what was termed a *dust bed*. This perhaps was made from the fluffy rolls of wool dust that gathered under the loom, caused by the friction of the frames moving the warp yarns up and down and the added scraping of the beater on the warp yarns as it moved back and forth beating the weft yarn. Although not very substantial in loft, the short wool fibers that dropped to the floor may have provided at least some degree of warmth.

A *pallet* was the least type of mattress and was simply a "poor" or a "mean bed" of ticking or rough woven tow linen filled with straw. Sometimes a *form*, which was a shaped mattress stuffed with straw for a support under a featherbed and was also sometimes used on a low or trundle bed, is listed with bed furnishings.

Pillows

BOLSTER

A *bolster* was a large, elongated sort of pillow. Either flat or tubular, it extended from side to side at the head end of the bed and was used as a base support for the actual down-filled pillows. The bolster was filled with straw or something firm. It was covered with linen ticking or a coarse linen cover. The ticking, or cover, measured roughly fifty-six to sixty-two inches long by sixteen to seventeen inches wide

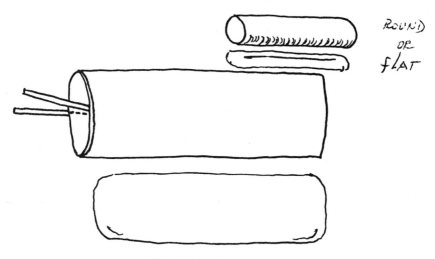

BOLSTERS AND COVER

Some bolsters were round and sausagelike in shape while others, from three to five inches thick, were flat. Made the width of the bed, they were covered with coarse tow linen or bedtick and cased with plaid, checked, or plain white linen. The closed end was seamed from inside; the open end hemmed with ties sewn on for tying.

92

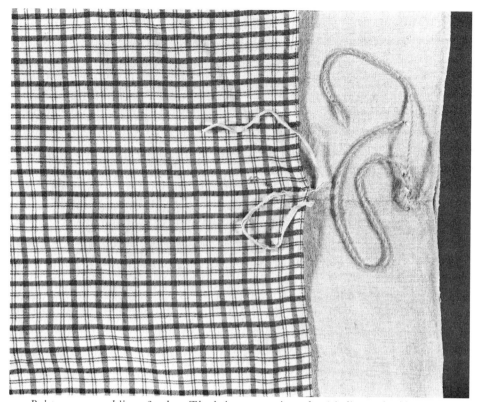

Bolster cover and linen fire bag. The bolster cover is made of indigo and white plaid linen with woven tape tie and a no. 6 or 9 embroidered 7½-inch piece added at one end for length. Handsewn throughout. Total measurement: 59½ inches by 19 inches. From Exeter, New Hampshire.

The fire bag is woven of rough, natural-color tow linen. Fire bags were used like buckets to fight fires. They were made of tightly woven, heavy unbleached linen and held water well. The bag shown is seamed across the bottom and down the center front with a narrow hem at the top. The initials of its owner, "E. K.," are cross-stitched in indigo at back center. Dimensions are 57 inches by 19¾ inches. Circa 1790–1830. From Bantam, Connecticut.—Old Sturbridge Village photograph by Donald F. Eaton

when flattened, the opening being about thirty-three inches at one end, sewn together. This is not a standard measurement, but merely an approximation, as bolsters varied. Additional white linen bolster casings were used over the bolster cover.

Pillows were larger and more square-shaped than today's pillows. They were usually goosedown-filled, covered with pillow-ticking, and then covered in fine white linen casing, woven of single-ply linen. Usually two were placed side by side over the bolster.

Pillow Cases

Pillow-cases, pillow-beares, pillow-coates, and *pillow casings* were different names for the finely woven bleached white linen pillow cases, with two to four narrow linen twill ties on one end to keep pillows in place, measuring approximately 32–35 inches by 16–17 inches. They were finished with narrow ¼-inch hems. By 1850 the hems were a larger 1¼ inch or so and twill tape ties were, in some cases, replaced by four to five buttons and buttonholes. By the 1880s they were embroidered, trimmed with lace, and sometimes scalloped.

Pillows with their fine linen casings and bolsters with their outer white linen casings were not usually covered with the coverlet or quilt as we are apt to use a bedspread in the twentieth century. They were exposed with the sheeting turned back onto the blanket edge on the best bedsteads, especially in the rural areas. Very small and lesser low beds often lacked a pillow and white linen sheeting. It was common to find all linens for the bed woven of homespun linen until the late eighteenth century.

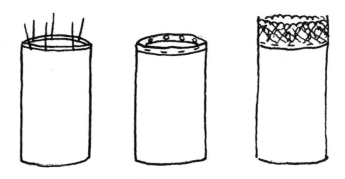

PILLOW CASINGS
Left: *With twill ties.* Center: *With buttons.* Right: *With lace trimming.*

Sheets

The same finely woven and bleached white linen was also used for sheeting. Woven of two forty- to forty-five-inch panels, with single-ply handspun linen, sheets were seamed in the center and finely hemmed at

94

the ends. The many fine linens used for bed sheeting, pillow casings, bed hangings and curtains, as well as table linens, were cherished, hard-earned possessions and became more lovely with age. Some bed hangings and sheeting from the early eighteenth century are still amazingly supple and glow with the soft sheen that only use and age impart to linen. Sheets were embroidered, usually cross-stitch, at center top near the seam with a number and sometimes initials. The numbers were an effective method of rotating their use. This tradition persisted into the nineteenth century.

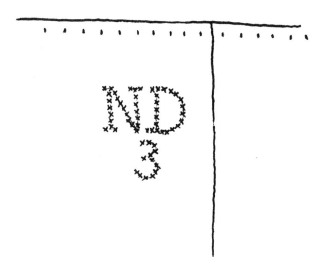

IDENTIFICATION EMBROIDERED ON SHEET

A sheet of two panels, each with a width of 40½ inches and a ⅛-inch turned bottom hem, was woven of homespun linen by Ruth Hardy Ropes Prince of Wenham in 1811. It is initialed near the top ⅞-inch hem in cross-stitch with her number 8. The sheet is now in the Wenham Historical Society collection, Wenham, Massachusetts.

Hempen linen is a coarser linen that was also used for sheeting and is listed as "hempen" and "hampen sheting." This was woven from flax not as carefully prepared and combed as for the very finest woven linens. It had not been bleached white, but was cream-colored.

Listed in early seventeenth-century inventories of the Plymouth,

Massachusetts area are items of bed furnishings, including many of the types discussed above:

Plymouth	1633	Eaton Carpenter: "1 old bedstead & fforme, 2 curtines & a rod"
Plymouth	1633	Will Wright: along with a great many other items including bedsteads and furnishings in several rooms, "One old halfe headed bedstead—1 old bagge of ffeathers"
Plymouth	1634	Thomas Evans: "one canvas bed with fethers . . . 6 bever skins, oter skins, a seal skin. . . ." (Author's note: Since he listed only a few other small items, he may have used a skin or two as blankets and may have been a trapper.)
Scituate	1639	Thomas Pryor: "In the chamber . . . 1 flock bed, 1 flock boulster, 1 feather pillow & 2 blanketts"
Scituate	1639	Mr. Willin Gilson: "Three feather beds with sheets & blanketting to them . . . one smale flock bed wth linnen & woolen to yt + a boulster"
Scituate	1641	Nathaniel Tilden: "One bed furnished, three paires of sheetes and two pair of pillowcoates"
Duxburrows (Duxbury)	1641	William Kempe: "1 feather bed + two pillows, 3 white blankets, 1 Blew Rugg [bed rug], 1 pillow case . . . in the Kitchen chamber—1 flock bedd and two boulsters"

Outer Coverings

COVERLETS

"Coverlet" is an old word that brings to mind the patterned coverlets woven of indigo and white in overshot designs. However, the word "coverlet" in earliest colonial times represented several forms and meanings. As a general term it simply meant the top, outer covering of the bedstead, be it a quilt, counterpane, or patterned woven overshot cover. The word took its meaning from the French words, dating as far back as 1301—"*couvre*" (cover) and "*lit*" (bed). We find it itemized in inventories with many spellings: *coverlet, coverlid, coverlett, courlead, courlet,* and as early as 1465, in an early English will, as "a coverlyte of whyte."

Woven patterned coverlets were of the overshot, double-weave, and summer and winter varieties.

Overshot. These coverlets have an early history in New England, evolving from table linen or napery patterns of the seventeenth century and from the napery traditions of England, Scotland, and Ireland. The many napery white-on-white patterns, and especially those with floating threads patterning the design, slowly became used in combination with wool. One small block coverlet pattern in a weaver's draft book dates from 1723. Small geometric designs such as "birdseye" were used, first as woolen patterns in woven shawls, then gradually as coverlet patterns. This came about as the patterns were enlarged and the floating woolen yarns became the colored wool pattern on a linen ground—or the *overshot* coverlet pattern. Earliest coverlet patterns were relatively small, simple repeat designs and continued to use the linen warp. One of the earliest known coverlets was woven in 1720 by Mrs. Benjamin Henry of Halifax, Vermont, just north of Leyden over the Massachusetts border. The pattern resembles "Jefferson's Fancy" in its alternating squares of sunrise and simple groups of blocks. Patterns growing larger and incorporating varied other geometric motifs in the late eighteenth and early nineteenth centuries were sometimes woven on a cotton warp, if a cotton mill was near and the farmwife could afford to buy the mill-spun yarn. Eventually the designs grew larger into tables of repeated geometrics. Larger areas of ground surrounded and interlaced with complicated, detailed groupings evolved as the *double weave* and *summer and winter weave.*

Double Weave. This coverlet was equally beautiful on both sides. One side had relatively large areas that were predominantly dark ground with light designs. The other side had a predominantly light (usually white) ground with dark designs. The pattern was the same on both sides, but simply reversed light and dark. This was achieved by actually creating two layers of material while weaving one. The two layers were joined by the edges of the pattern itself, but in the areas of solid design, the layers could be pulled apart when picked up with the fingers. Some of the fancy double weaves would have had to be woven on multiharnessed looms, such as a professional weaver would have, but there are simpler patterns which are known to have been woven at home by experienced weavers. Since there are weavers today who are proficient enough to handweave such coverlets, certainly this weave cannot be eliminated from the home weavers' accomplishments.

Summer and Winter Weave. This weave at first glance could be mistaken for the double weave. It, too, has equally reversed patterns. Because it has a dark ground (winter) with light pattern on one side and a light ground (summer) with dark pattern on the other side, it can be confused with the double weave. Its revealing identity is in the ground. Unlike the overshot, which has comparatively small areas of background because of the practical limits to its floating yarns, the summer and winter is capable of large areas of ground. And unlike the double weave, the large areas of ground cannot be separated, but rather the pattern yarn is there, incorporated in the finely woven ground. A knowing close examination with the naked eye is all that is needed to identify.

For more than 100 years prior to the invention of the Jacquard loom, handwoven coverlets made on the four-harness barn-frame loom were based on the block, rose, and lozenge shape geometrics. For about two hundred years, from the late seventeenth to the late nineteenth centuries, these continued to be woven in the remote agricultural communities and isolated upland farms. Traditional patterns repeatedly are in evidence. These were passed on in a family, generation to generation. Sometimes they were exchanged with another farmwife. And new patterns and variations were introduced to villagers by the professional weaver.

With the increased population of the itinerant and community weavers (see chapter 2), more patterns and fancier designs were available to the farmwife, who could now select a new pattern from the itinerant. Spring would come and with it the itinerant weaver. He would set up his loom in a house or a shop in the village. The women would bring their dyed wool, spun the winter before, and select from his pattern books of fresh, new fascinating coverlet designs. The farmwife would pay him to weave one or barter with some needed commodity that he could trade. He now did the work of setting up, dressing the loom, and weaving that she had done before. If he lived temporarily at a farm, he would weave in exchange for room and meals and odd jobs to help the farmer. He could, using his far more complicated loom with its multiple harnesses, weave birds, flowers, and fancy borders, often designing the owner's name and date into the border. Proud owners of heirloom patterned coverlets are sometimes saddened to learn that the coverlet they had been led to believe was woven by great great-grand-mother was probably woven by the itinerant weaver. However, she may well have washed, carded, and spun the yarn herself. If the yarn is single-ply, it may have been homespun and home dyed. If double-ply, it could have been purchased at the nearest mill, many of which sprang up in New England after 1800. However, in spite of the itinerant weavers' availability, until after the Civil War the simpler traditional patterns were still woven at home on the farm.

Coverlet Pattern Names. Many coverlets have pattern names, which vary according to heritage, region, or locale. The weaver's imagination, skill, and creative abilities probably extended into naming patterns, too. As with a cooking recipe, a woman is apt to experiment and be creative in her own way, so it was with the designing and naming of coverlets. Names are fascinating in their lore and whimsey—Sno-Ball, Chariots, Lover's Knot, Granite State, Queen's Delight. There are literally hundreds of names and variations of traditional designs.

To attribute a coverlet pattern to any particular region is misleading as the patterns were woven with minor and major variations. They might still be given the same name, or an entirely new name, depending on the whim of the weaver or the regional historical significance at the time. Some traditional patterns are repeatedly found and easily recognizable; but some were altered and combined with other pattern motifs, leading to confusion of identity. Many were also carried south and west and were renamed. To show the scope of just one weaver's collection, Alice Morse Earle wrote in 1898 of a patterns list compiled by "Weaver Rose" of Kingston, Rhode Island that included those nearly 100 years old (at that time). Weaver Rose was later known to have woven over 300 patterns (see Village or Public Weavers in chapter 2). Keeping in mind that he gathered patterns from many sources as well as created some of his own, we find the following a picturesque group:

99

Chariot-wheels and Church Windows
Church-steps
Bachelor's fancy
Devil's fancy
Five doves in a row
Shooting-star
Rising sun
Rail fence
Green veils
Whig Rose

Perry's Victory
Lady Washington's Fancy
Orange-Peel
All Summer and All Winter
Bricks and Blocks
Capus Diaper
Dutch tulip
Rose in bloom
Pansies in the Wilderness
Five Snowballs

How Coverlets Were Sewn and Used. Coverlets were woven most often of 42-inch to 45-inch width material. The full length of the material required was approximately twice as long as the bed the coverlet was to be used on, as it was made of two panels. The total length of patterned material was cut from the loom and then divided into the two panels. The design was then precisely matched, placing panels side by side, and carefully sewn together with tiny, firm stitches. The seam, running straight up the center, is usually not hard to find on old coverlets. The top and bottom were finished with a narrow ⅜-inch turned hem, with tiny hemming stitches.

It was not customary, as it is today, to have two or more beds in the same room covered with matching coverlets. They were usually of varying patterns and different colors. Needless to say, these patterned coverlets were woven for beds, not wing chairs and sofas.

We owe a great deal of our present-day knowledge of how coverlets were woven to the craftswomen of the southern Appalachians who kept coverlet weaving alive in the early twentieth century, when few other parts of the country had an interest in weaving. Their folkways continued for generations. Allen Eaton wrote in 1937 in *Handicrafts of the Southern Highlands* that the continuation of folkways in the mountains often was more easily traced, since a large majority of the inhabitants were of English, Scottish, and Irish ancestry and because of their isolation kept their culture relatively pure. He quotes a poem by Ann Cobb in her book *Kinfolks*, noting a heritage from Scotland:

> I recollect my granny at the loom,
> Weaving the blue one yonder on the bed.
> She put the shuttle by and laid in tomb.

East bed chamber of the Fenno house. All-wool quilted indigo coverlet on pencil post bed. Two shades of indigo wool used for warp and weft. The coverlet is quilted with simple center pattern and a geometric border on drop; its backing is of coarse roughly woven woolen. The half-curtain is a single panel of linen with self-tab loops sliding over the wooden rod. When closed, curtain just barely covers window. Note the early period William and Mary highboy with hatboxes and the blue wool cushion on chair. Coverlet and curtain date from circa 1790–1810.—Old Sturbridge Village photograph by Donald F. Eaton

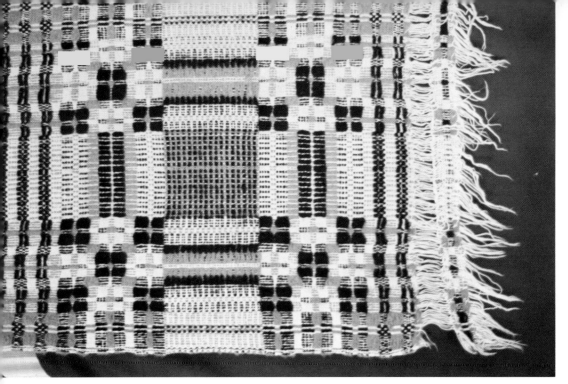

Handwoven coverlet, in black and butterscotch wool, with fringe woven, not applied. Two-ply white cotton warp, with handspun two-ply wool pattern yarns. Wool is redyed yarn unraveled from "footlins" (socks with worn-out feet). The coverlet was handwoven of handspun wool by Dulcena Dewey in Stark, New Hampshire, circa 1850.
—Photograph by Philip D. Bogdonoff courtesy Miss Ruth Montgomery

Home-woven coverlet, in the early small overshot pattern, showing similarity to table linen weaves. Woven of homespun and home-dyed single-ply woolen. Blue and gold, with wool background weft of tabby. Warp is single-ply linen. Lined with a fine linsey-woolsey of plain weave, also homespun natural wool and linen. This coverlet is among the earliest home-woven on the Gifford Saconesset farm, and dates from the middle to late eighteenth century.—Photograph by Philip D. Bogdonoff courtesy The Saconesset Homestead Museum, West Falmouth (Cape Cod), Massachusetts

Home-woven quilted coverlet of the eighteenth century. The top layer is woven of very fine homespun indigo wool in a plain weave. It has a filler of lamb's wool (see opening where worn) and a backing of coarser handspun wool in wider sett plain weave. The coverlet is quilted with linen thread through the filler, catching the lining layer.—Photograph by Philip D. Bogdonoff courtesy The Saconesset Homestead Museum, West Falmouth (Cape Cod), Massachusetts

Bed rug by Mary Comstock. Needleworked in running stitch of uncut pile on what was once a plaid blanket woven in bird's-eye twill pattern. Where pile has worn off the diamond effect shows the blanket foundation. Generally dark in appearance, the background pile is brown and black; the pattern pile blue, tan, and brown. Width: 78 inches; length: 87 inches.

The rug is signed by Mary herself: "Mary Comstock's Rug Jany 30 1810." Mary was married to Daniel Comstock of Norwich, Connecticut, and settled in Shelburne in what became Comstock Point (now Shelburne Point), Vermont.—Photograph by John M. Miller courtesy Shelburne Museum

Bed rug initialed "E. L.," maker not known. Needleworked in running stitch with cut pile. Worn places have been reworked with uncut pile to preserve pattern. Foundation is of rough-spun natural wool in plain weave. Made in two panels seamed vertically. Width: 94 inches; length: 100 inches. The rug was made in the Connecticut River Valley circa 1807.—Photograph by John M. Miller courtesy Shelburne Museum

Handwoven, home-dyed blanket of linsey-woolsey with warp of handspun linen and weft stripes of assorted color in handspun single-ply wool. Both linen and wool were raised on the Dewey farm. The colors are red, indigo, brown, and pink with natural white wool. The two panels are center-seamed and hemmed at both ends with a ⅜-inch turn. Dulcena Dewey of Stark, New Hampshire made this blanket circa 1850.
—Photograph by Philip D. Bogdonoff courtesy Miss Ruth Montgomery

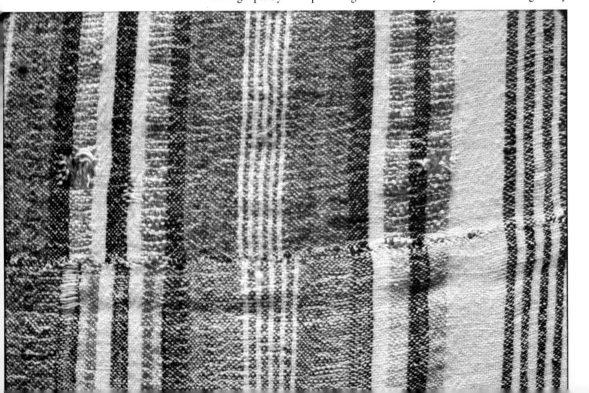

Her word was I could claim hit when I wed.
"Flower of Edinboro" was hits name,
Betokening the land from which she came.

Eaton's book and others with the colorful work of the Appalachian craftswomen photographed, and pattern drafts, are well worth looking into, if one is interested in pursuing the art of coverlet weaving. Books containing pattern drafts are marked with an asterisk in the Bibliography. Records kept by professional or itinerant weavers are also invaluable sources of patterns.

Miss Ruth Montgomery of Norway, Maine, has a farm coverlet woven out of "footlins." Footlins were cast-off knitted stockings, which were saved, then unraveled, respun, and redyed and used for the color-pattern yarn of the heirloom coverlet.

The coverlet of yellow and black (the black dye was expertly set) has been documented as having been woven by Miss Montgomery's aunt, who lived on the farm in Stark, New Hampshire, where as late as 1880 all weaving for the household was done by her with homespun linen and wool raised on that farm. Miss Montgomery, who now resides in Maine, claims that this particular coverlet was used by her grandfather, who worked in a logging camp in New Hampshire and rolled up in it at night to sleep. This is a heavy and firmly woven coverlet. The remaining fringe is a sign of the period. Fringes were added to fancy woven coverlets from about 1850 on and appeared in the bed hangings and testers of the same period. This fringe was ingeniously woven as the coverlet weaving progressed. The coverlet is typical of the expert traditional weaving carried on in rural areas, and evidence of how late the tradition survived in the inland remote areas among farming families.

BED RUG

The bed rug was a homewoven and homesewn shaggy ruglike covering used in severely cold weather as the topmost layer of bedding. Although a kind of coverlet, the bed rug was often listed along with a coverlet, but differentiated as a "rugg." It was used in the seventeenth, eighteenth, and early nineteenth centuries. A bed rug valued at two shillings, sixpence was listed in the Plymouth Godbertson inventory of 1633.

Godfrey Dearborn of Hampton, New Hampshire, in his will, dated 1680, gave his wife liberty "to dispose of . . . one fether bed & boulster & rug & coverlett & her greatt Bible & her Red flannel petticoat."

The bed rug was usually listed in the context of bed furnishings as simply a "rugg." The floor rug came much later.

The word "rug" has several derivations: Middle English *rugen*, *ruggen*; Old Norwegian *rögg*, meaning tuft, shagginess; Swedish *rugg*, meaning entangled hair; Norwegian dialect *rugga*, a coarse rug.

Once thought to have been an extreme rarity, bed rugs are now believed to have been an important inclusion in the total bed furnishings. Not only are they listed in seventeenth-century inventories, but evidence of a number of existing rugs is gradually appearing. Earliest New England bed rugs are thought to have been plain, or perhaps motley. In Will Wright's inventory of 1633 he listed: "In the Bed chamber . . . 2 rugges, 1 green one & one white one," and in the context of old, used bed items he listed: "One little ffock bed & an old fether bolster, with a pre of worne sheets, an old greene rugge." The same will mentioned "in the loft over the first room, 1 old bagge of ffeathers, 1 old white rugge, 2 hogsheads & a barrell." Thus Will Wright possessed four rugs, all seemingly plain: an old and newer green, and an old and newer white.

The Plymouth Godbertson will of 1633 lists "3 white ruggs & 3 pr blankets [valued at] 01.00.00."

Christopher Joce of Portsmouth in 1676 willed to his daughters three beds with rugs, all listed again in the context of bed furnishings, but not giving colors, as follows: "to tho: Sevy's corn-field, as also a ffeather bed wth bolster, Pillowes, sheets, Blankets & Rugg . . . I give my daughter Margaret 8 acres of land . . . a ffeather bed, Bolster, Pillowes, sheets, blankets & rugg, + 30 pounds. Unto my daughter Mary I give . . . as also a ffeather bed wth like furniture as her sisters and pasturing for one cow."

Thomas Beard of Dover, New Hampshire willed to his son Thomas in 1678 "the featherbed wth blankets sheets bolster + pilloes + rugg there unto belonging wch is in the parlor."

Along with two cows, John Heard, Dover, willed his daughter Dorcas in 1687 "the fether bed & bedstead with the bolsters & pillers rugg blanket & what cloth belong to it which is now called by the name of Dorcase bed."

A number of eighteenth-century patterned bed rugs of Connecticut origin have been found. However, two of the earliest existing bed rugs are from North Andover, Massachusetts (1722), and Ipswich, Massachusetts (1724). The tradition of working in the maker's initials and year made seems, even at that early time, to have been a well-established custom, as well as the tradition of a defined rectangular area for the top of the bed, with the border area designed separately. In later bed rugs the center and border areas are not as clearly defined. It is interesting to note that while most bed rugs adhere to another tradition of floral design, the highly stylized but simple design of the early Ipswich rug made by Catherine Thorn is unusual in its incorporation of two horses and two roosters as well as hearts and flowers. One other rug dated circa 1775–1800 with no initials, from the Connecticut River Valley area, has what seems to be a few birds. But on close count its design incorporates twenty-one birds of various sizes! These two examples at least seem to have been more independent in design.

The weighty bed rug was made of a cut loop pile similar in appearance, at first glance, to a shaggy hooked rug. However, the technique used for the loops was not a hooking, but a sewing one. Bed rugs were constructed of a foundation backing on which the loops were worked. The foundation textile was a home-woven plain or twill weave of all wool, all linen, or linsey-woolsey, sometimes of blanket origin, and sewn together in two or three vertical panels. The loops were thought to have been worked on the completed foundation off the loom. Although the technique seems similar to that used to make the *ryijy* (meaning rug in Finnish), which was used in Scandinavia for beds and wall hangings, the seventeenth- and eighteenth-century American rug was made differently. It was probably worked with a large curved needle, possibly of bone or wood, similar to a roping needle, using a sewing stitch in and out which formed standing loops on the top, or right side, and visible running stitches on the reverse side. The loops on top were cut to form a pile, although some loops were often deliberately left uncut. This is not quite like the Scandinavian rug, which required many individual Turkish-type knots to be tied across the width of the warp while still on the loom, and then the shuttle thrown with weft or filler yarn binding in the knot. In the *ryijy*, these alternating knotting and weaving rows continued the desired length of the rug while under tension on the loom.

Generally, the patterns of American bed rugs in existence are deep-colored grounds, such as indigos, browns, or greens, with bright-colored meandering vine borders, curling leaves, and stylized aster-carnation type florals in bold designs. All have their own individual design patterns, but many seem to have come from some common source. From the earliest, thought to have been plain, the patterns went to geometrics worked with a center oblong, with wide geometric repeat in the borders, which dropped over the sides of the bed. Later, from 1750 into the nineteenth century, the adaptations of the tree-of-life design were influential in the patterns of bed rugs. Another pattern type popular after 1775 was the widely stylized center floral design with meandering branches and large leaves balanced in the traditional oblong center, bordered with vinelike repeated motifs. However, there are still other bed rugs with no border at all and the complete foundation used as one well-balanced design area. The finishing edges of the rugs were usually simply bound flat on the reverse side. A few rugs have been found with narrow fringe sewn on, though this was not generally common.

Considering that the bed rug was made from a home-woven foundation or blanket, of tufts dyed and spun of home-grown wool, it seems likely to this author that the yarns for the loops came from the end pieces of the weaver's loom; this wasted warp, which could not be woven, could amount to a considerable quantity if saved from each warp by the end of a year's weaving. And, as other weavers would agree, such a procedure would have been an apt application for otherwise wasted yarns and not out of keeping with the New England housewife's thrift. These eight- to ten-inch lengths of *thrums*, as they are called, could conceivably be grouped, four or five ends in a roping, and used in a roping needle, to be drawn or sewn into the foundation for loops. The hypothesis that the thrums were used in rugs or carpets is supported by a quotation of 1519 in the Oxford English Dictionary: "The bandy thrummys of the carpettis toke me fast by the feete," meaning the gay, lively colorings of the thrums kept my feet firmly fixed (to admire). "Carpettis" is further defined by the Oxford English Dictionary in a description by La Crusca as "a coarse hanging for a table, made of rough woollen materials, and of patches of motley colors." The verb to *thrum* is also given this meaning: "to furnish or adorn with thrums or ends of thread; to cover with thrums or small tufts, raise a pile upon [cloth]; *to make shaggy*." Continuing from the Oxford English Dictionary: "Shag—a garment, rug, or mat of. shaggy material." And a reference is made to "shagge" and "white rugge" along with thrums: "1664—Power—a [magnified] sage leaf looks like white rugge, or shagge, full of knots, tassel'd all with white silver thrums." Supposing that a large batch of thrums were deliberately collected over a long period to use and perhaps redye for sewing in a bed rug, the finished rug might well show the variance in dyes after several centuries. This would explain the background dye variances of one color in a number of bed rugs.

COUNTERPANES

Counterpanes were single-layer, unlined spreads, usually made of finely woven single-ply linen or fine woolen twill, often with light airy embroidery—usually bright colors worked on a white, black, or indigo ground. Some were delightful with flowers, birds, animals, and vines, in charmingly simple and open patterns. These spreads were creative expressions of the rural New England woman's adaptation to her environment and evinced her freedom of choice and design. Another ingenious example of a counterpane is shown in the drawing of part of a finely woven white twill blanket with crosslines of blue forming large squares. Alternate open squares are embroidered with highly stylized floral sprigs in bright-colored wool.

Plaid counterpanes were one of the most colorful types of bed coverings. Woven of single-ply wool in twill, usually using a traditional tartan or sometimes an improvised plaid, they were like an extralarge blanket covering the bed. The one illustrated in the accompanying photograph is at the Shelburne Museum, Vermont. It is in red, white,

Folding bedstead with curtains of medium blue and white plaid linen in a plain weave. The woolen coverlet is woven in twill with cardinal red and white plaid and a blue crossline. When space was needed, the bed folded up into the curtained area and the linen curtains were drawn together to conceal the bedding. This bed is in the children's garret at the Dutton house. Curtains were adapted from a patchwork quilt.—Photograph by John M. Miller courtesy Shelburne Museum

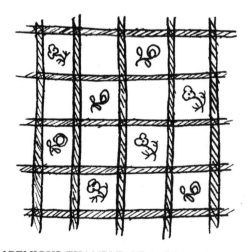

INGENIOUS EXAMPLE OF A COUNTERPANE

and blue tartan and is used with an equally handsome blue and white plaid linen bed curtain on a half-headed bedstead. The total effect is compelling.

Note: See Decorated Bed Furnishings later in this chapter, for additional counterpanes.

COARSE COVERLID

Used on low, folding, and other lesser-type beds was a crude type of coverlet woven of roughly spun woolen yarn in plain weave, sometimes dyed, or in natural sheep's grays or browns. It was simply tucked in around the foot and sides of the bed.

Along with other bedding, Joseph Gooch of Milton, Massachusetts in 1770 lists "in back chamber '1 course lid.'" He also lists "in East chamber '1 conterpain.'"

QUILTS

Quilts in their earliest form appear often in inventories as "quilted counterpanes" and "quilted coverlids." From the late seventeenth century they were called quilts. The tops were of such solid colors as indigo, olive, dark green, and butternut brown. The quilts themselves were made of three layers of materials: a closely woven dyed woolen for top, a filling of lamb's wool of washed short fibers not suitable for spinning, and a bottom layer of more open coarsely spun wool, dyed a different color from that of the top. Often the lining was a strong shade of yellow ochre or gold, sometimes, perhaps, the result of fading from red. The three layers were sewn together and then quilted in a pattern, using linen thread that closely matched the color of the top layer. The quilting pattern is seen by reversing the "quilted coverlid," plainly showing the darker threads as they caught all three layers. Other types of material used for quilt tops, which are not to be confused with the finely home-woven tops, are the glazed, heat-treated, imported fabrics—camblet and calamanco—that have a luster or sheen. Whereas the filling and backing may have been homemade, the top of camblet or calamanco would have been rather costly, and is found documented in wealthier homes. The earliest quilting patterns are relatively open-

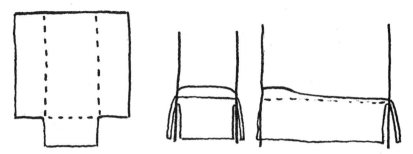

QUILTED SOLID-COLOR EIGHTEENTH-CENTURY COVERLET
The bases were attached at the sides and fell almost to the floor. The cut-out area allowed for bed posts at the foot end.

spaced and simple. In the mid and late eighteenth century, when there was less urgency of survival and more time to devote to needlework, the designs were more intricate and varied. The tree-of-life patterns of balanced vines and leaves and flowers, along with the pineapple motif, became popular. The colors used for these quilts were deep shades of bottle green, olive greens, ochres, browns, and the ever reliable indigo. Later, when cochineal dye became available, there were lovely pinky rose and rosy reds. Often the bed hangings were dyed to match. Although the quilted coverlets are sometimes called "linsey-woolsey," upon close examination they are usually seen to be three layers of wool and contain no linen, as the name would imply. Even the imported camblet and calamanco glazed tops were woven of worsted wool before glazing. However, the bed hangings often were of genuine linsey-woolsey, dyed to match.

The quilts of little patches sewn together that we are more familiar with today were first made in the latter half of the eighteenth century, when printed cottons were beginning to be available, and the used and worn blankets and sheets could be put into new use as fillings and linings. Since it was not until the late eighteenth century that the Yankee peddler began to carry the printed textiles on his wagon, and since he was one of the inland rural housewife's few contacts with the new vogues, quilting with a variety of colorful pieces of printed fabric did not become common in farming households until the late eighteenth and early nineteenth centuries, and even then, patches of home-woven fabric were sewn into early quilts. There were peddlers who had a single specialty, and printed calico was one. This required a wagon with rolls of cloth packed on the floor; the sides of the wagon held rods with which to display the rolls, one above the other, when the time came for the women to select and purchase. The sides had flaps that would fold down in bad weather or while traveling from village to village. To the farmwife who spun, carded, dyed, and wove most of her household and family textiles it must have been a joy to see the wagon coming—and a dilemma to decide which among the tiny imported prints she could afford, if only for a dress for herself and daughters or perhaps curtains for the parlor. Then even the tiniest scraps from such sewing projects would be carefully put aside and saved for pieces in a future quilt. The earliest prints had dark grounds and were methodically planned into quilts, using many types of white textiles for white ground in the quilt. Calicoes and other prints became more plentiful and varied when available through village dry-goods stores as well as the peddler in the late eighteenth and early nineteenth centuries. The many beautiful patched quilts are a subject separate from this study, other than as mentioned. They can be investigated through the many museums and colorful books of recent and past publication on the subject.

Blankets

Blankets were a mainstay of colonial beds, whether great beds or a low bed of the most humble farmer. Blankets were used as "woolen sheeting" when linen sheets were not available.

In early Plymouth records they were listed along with bed rugs. In 1633, Samuel Fuller the Elder listed "3 white ruggs & 3 pr. blanckets." In 1641, William Kempe listed "2 white blanketts + 1 old greene rugg," and in the kitchen chamber, "3 white blankets." Their frequency and number increased as home weaving enlarged their inventories, and blankets appear in constant repetition in every household listing, usually with at least two or three to a bed. Itemized simply as a "woolen blancket," the natural cream white wool in twill weave seems to have been most common. This plain white blanket was used along with linsey-woolsey striped and plain blankets, or later in the eighteenth century under the checkered, plain, or embroidered top blanket. Some lesser beds never knew a coverlet, quilt, or spread, and were simply made with a colorful plaid or check top blanket, or even plain rough wool, as cover.

Blankets, regardless of color or design, were traditionally woven in two panels, seamed neatly at the center with tiny overcast stitches and hemmed with a narrow one-quarter-inch roll. Early plaid blankets are often found with a hem-stitched fringe at one end, and turned hem at the other. This would suggest that the fringed end was turned back several inches at the top of the bed as a decorative effect when the blanket was used as the only top cover.

Generally blankets, while varying in colors and styles, were woven basically in four weaves: tabby, or plain weave; a diagonal twill weave which made a denser more durable blanket; a bird's-eye twill weave of concentric diamonds, often placed with checks in between for an inter-

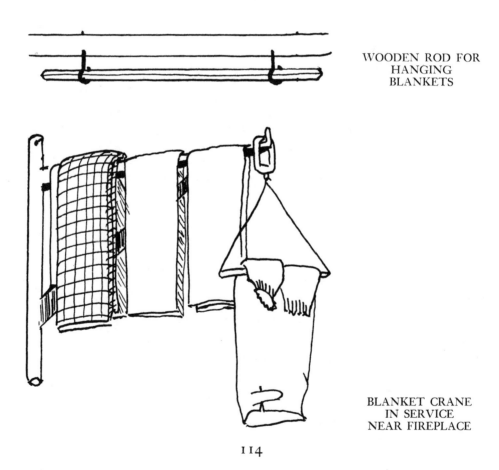

WOODEN ROD FOR
HANGING
BLANKETS

BLANKET CRANE
IN SERVICE
NEAR FIREPLACE

esting and striking effect, and the blanket or basket weave with all its variations.

LINSEY-WOOLSEY BLANKETS

These were true to the name, having a very fine single-ply white linen warp set very close, and a fine woolen weft. In some of the remote areas the wool weft would be coarser. These linen and wool blankets were lighter in feel and weight than those of all wool and were used along with the heavier blanket or alone as a light summer blanket. These were common in all white or with 1- to 2½-inch-wide stripes of natural brown wool or indigo, alternated with white stripes. Evidence has been found that summer blankets of cotton warp with fine white wool weft were made in Rhode Island as early as 1834, when cotton became available at the mills. An unusually colorful blanket was woven in plain weave on fine linen warp with a great variety of stripes in all manner of colors from reds and pink to browns and indigos, completely omitting white stripes (see bottom photograph on p. 104). This random-striped blanket was woven by Dulcena Dewey in the last half of the nineteenth century in Stark, New Hampshire. She also wove a baby boy's blanket that is unusual and handsome in plain weave with alternating ⅜-inch stripes of sheep's brown, red, and orange on a very fine linen warp. She raised, spun, and dyed the yarns. These blankets are further evidence of an early tradition that persisted late into the nineteenth century.

CHECKED, CROSSLINE, AND PLAID BLANKETS

Checks of indigo blue, mustard, and brown were early colors, while red, orange, and green were later colors as these dyes became available. They were woven in plain weave or twill of all wool. Sometimes checks were woven in geometric weave of concentric goose-eye or bird's-eye twill, such as surviving Shaker blankets. These were not solely Shaker in design, however, but rather refined and well-balanced designs that were traditional to both Shakers and "the world's people."

Crosslines and windowpane check were also popular woven in plain weave, using less of the dyed wool with greater areas of white than the check allowed. These were also usually of all wool, but sometimes incorporated cotton warps and crosslines. Perhaps the most colorful blankets were the lively plaids of indigos, golds, browns, and reds, revealing Scottish heritage. Some were tartans or adaptations of tartans and others were designed utilizing those yarns and dyes available. Color combinations are often unusual and bright.

On a bed in the Crownenshield Bentley house in Salem, Massachusetts is a cream white and blue crossline 1½-inch windowpane check blanket, woven in single-ply wool in twill weave by Keziah Jenks in 1794. It measures 85 inches by 77 inches with ⅜-inch hems top and bottom and the cross-stitched initials "KJ."

A brown plaid blanket, circa 1840, of homespun home-dyed single-ply butterscotch and dark brown wool was woven by Mrs. Abram (Olive) Prescott. The colors for the yarn were made from a species of lichen, scraped from rocks in the woods and pastures near her home. Olive Prescott was the wife of Captain Prescott, from Forge Village, Massachusetts. The blanket is now in the Essex Institute, Salem, Massachusetts.

EMBROIDERED BLANKETS

Perhaps these could be considered in the coverlet class. The embroidered blankets of the late eighteenth and early nineteenth centuries were usually creamy white wool, although sometimes found in dark or pastel colors. These were used for show and often were large enough to cover the pillow. Colored yarns used in their tracery were worked into center and narrow border designs. Often crudely executed, their naive but delightful floral, star compass, and sun motifs gave a very feminine look to otherwise utilitarian blankets. These were thought to have been used on beds in warmer weather in place of the heavier, warmer coverlet.

BEARING BLANKETS

These were traditionally bright red and were small blankets of fine wool to wrap infants. The earliest settlers of Plymouth perhaps referred to imported bearing blankets when listing "red bearing blankets," but the tradition persisted into the eighteenth century. Bearing blankets were undoubtedly woven at home, used for one child after another, and passed from one generation to the next.

Bed Hangings

The early New England farming communities, isolated and provincial, were permeated with home traditions from England, Scotland, Ireland, and Europe. They clung to the familiar habits and modes of living generation after generation. The forms of life in the New World were deeply influenced by the traditions of the Old, as was evident in their beds and bed furnishings. The great bed with all its furnishings persisted in use in rural areas into the nineteenth century, being willed father to son again and again. Its curtains still provided comfort from the chills of ever drafty houses. And persisting along with the great bed was the half-headed bedstead with its curtains that closed when the bed folded up. Low beds were also in steady and common use rurally, sometimes with bed curtains suspended from a frame on a cord hanging by an overhead hook, or even hung from exposed ceiling beams by means of drawstring and nails or hooks. Genre prints and paintings of Europe and England spanning two to three centuries are evidence of these long accepted and continuing modes.

SIDE VIEW OF THE
GREAT BED WITH
CURTAINS, VALANCE,
AND BASES

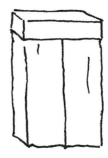

HALF-HEADED BEDSTEAD

Left: *Side view with bed down.* Right: *Frontal view with bed turned up against wall and curtains closed.*

117

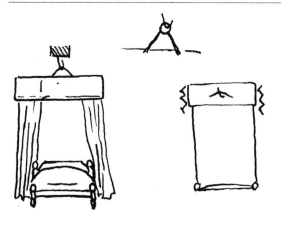

FRONTAL AND TOP VIEWS OF LOW BED

The valance and curtains are hung from a frame on a cord suspended from an overhead hook in a beam.

CRUDE CURTAIN ARRANGEMENT FOR LOW BED (Side View)

The curtains and valance may have been hung by nails from overhead beams to provide some degree of warmth and privacy.

Some of the more well-to-do country folk made note of a change in bed styles in the mid- to late eighteenth century by removing the base and the foot curtains from the great bed, which exposed the end posts. The valance, head cloth, and head end curtains remained. Sometimes the bed and curtains were caught with a tieback.

After the late eighteenth century the quilted coverlet or counterpane was made long enough to eliminate the former base (see Base and Flounce, below), but in some cases the bed curtains continued in use into the nineteenth century, and often with the foot curtains as well. Many rural adaptations of the popular empire style were applied, in the early nineteenth century, to the still used tester bed and arched canopy field bed. In one version of the tester bed the foot and side curtains, now narrower and gathered, were shortened to the length from the tester top to the approximate area of the bed rail. The head cloth was gathered and the side and foot curtains were caught back around the posts with a tieback or cord. A gathered valance, twenty inches deep

**FOUR-POST BED WITH
FOOT CURTAINS REMOVED**

*Removal of foot curtains
and bases exposed pencil posts
of bed though tester was still
covered with valance.*

**FOUR-POST BED WITH
LONG COUNTERPANE**

Note absence of base.

or more, was now set in, filling the open space on the tester frame between the curtains at the posts. The bed hangings now assumed a decorative instead of functional purpose. With a gathered flounce below and a white spread hanging to just below the flounce heading, the whole effect was changed, softer and more feminine.

Sometimes festoons were used on the tester or arched canopy bed. The valance, being shirred, was combined with the curtain, or the valance was draped or drawn up by rings and cords or drawstrings through the casing. These styles completely eliminated the long vertical side and foot end curtains, and decorated only the tester or canopy itself.

Sometimes the lower edge of the valance was cut to simulate the lines of festoons, and the edge was trimmed with cotton fringe to accentuate the shape.

Bed curtains in the seventeenth century and first half of the eighteenth century were usually listed as "hangings" or "curtains," meaning bed curtains, seldom window curtains. Bed curtains were listed under "bed and furnishings" and along with the head cloth and valance. As bed hangings they hung from a frame, or *tester*, which was supported by the four posts. The four-post flat-top bed, as it was known, was used well into the nineteenth century.

There were five pieces to the bed hangings: one *head cloth*, two *side head curtains*, and two *foot curtains*. These were usually edged with a narrow ⅛-inch hem.

SIDE VIEW OF THE
FOUR-POST BED IN THE
NINETEENTH CENTURY

*The head cloth and va-
lance are gathered and the side
and foot curtains caught back
to posts with tieback. The
flounce is gathered and carried
around the posts. No longer
designed to be pulled together,
the curtains serve a stylistic
function only.*

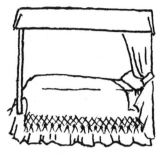

FOUR-POST BED WITH
FRINGED COVERLET

*In the midnineteenth cen-
tury, fringes were especially apt
to appear on coverlets in rural
areas. Those with time to make
them or money to buy them
already made used fringes to
adorn side bed curtains, valance,
flounce, and pillow casings.*

The *head cloth* was hung at the head end of the bed (that part of the bed nearest the wall), and was thought to have been fastened to the tester with tacks, or possibly in the eighteenth century by hooks using rings or loops.* Unlike the other four curtains, it was stationary. In the seventeenth and eighteenth centuries it was not gathered, but hung quite flat with only a slight easing. In the nineteenth century it was often gathered. It hung from the tester frame just to the horizontal head

---

* Do not take the descriptions in this book of rural styles and techniques used for window and bed hangings as pat formulas of "how-to's." Unfortunately, the only reliable evidence of just how rural hangings were hung and fastened to the bed consists of (1) the originals themselves, (2) pictorial documents, and (3) the books of cabinetmakers, who built the beds and designed the fashionable hangings for them, describing the latest styles from England and the continent. However, reaching one particular rule or theory becomes difficult as there are few original valances and hangings to examine, and they often vary or do not support one theory, thus raising more questions. Pictorial documents and folk art are valuable evidence of styles persisting in rural areas, but techniques are literally sketchy. The cabinetmakers' records are invaluable sources of information, but refer to the high-fashion styles of the wealthy. Even though they do set a commencing style date, it must be tempered by several decades' lag for rural areas, and a simpler adaptation to that style. Furthermore, firmly established traditions in some rural areas persisted long after the fashionable set had discarded them as being "old-fashioned." Thus, terminal dates cannot be clear-cut. Much surmising is therefore necessary.

Quilt from Ashbury, Massachusetts, of all woven wool, cut and sewn in the manner of a calico patchwork. Precisely executed in eight-pointed star. Colors are brown, ginger, olive, and medium-blue. The squares are solid pieced handwoven wool, quilted in fine stitches. The quilt has yellow backing, and is cut out at the sides of one end for fitting around bedposts. Dimensions are 92 by 98 inches.—Old Sturbridge Village photograph by Donald F. Eaton

Plaid blanket, woven in twill of single-ply homespun woolen, home-dyed. Early nineteenth century. Cranberry red, two shades of blue and brown. Panel is 81 by 37 inches, fringed at one end, with a ⅜-inch hem at the other end.

Photo is of one panel of three in the collection. Two panels show evidence of having been sewn together for a blanket, with the 3-inch blocks of plaid matching well. At a later period 4-inch hems were turned at one end; the other end remains fringed. The blanket was possibly used for a bed or door hanging.

The third panel is of particular interest for the evidence of a ¾-inch casing, sewn with cotton twist, formed at the top fold of what appears to have been a valance of approximately 8 inches. Both bottom edge and folded valance edge have a ⅜-inch turned hem, as do the other two panels. Possibly this third panel was used as part of a set of bed hangings. There is no fading such as might have resulted from its hanging at a window.—Photograph courtesy Merrimac Valley Textile Museum

Parlor of the Freeman farmhouse as it appeared circa 1820–1840. The window on walls of gay stenciling is curtained with cotton muslin shirred onto a rod. The curtain fabric was manufactured to give the effect of early textiles, and the style of the curtains is definitely of the period of the furnishings and wall decor. Shown in the photograph is the knotted style of hanging curtains used in warm weather, when windows were kept open. The big knots kept the curtains high, out of the dirt and dust that blew in from the barnyard. The stenciled chair is of the same period as the other furnishings in the room.—Old Sturbridge Village photograph by Donald F. Eaton

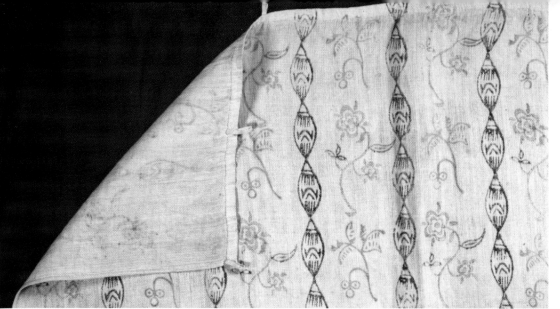

A single window curtain, stenciled, woven of single-ply linen with narrow ⅛-inch
twill tape loops sewn down into hem. Hem at top: ⅜ inch; bottom hem: ⅛ inch;
width: 29⅞ inches with ⅛-inch hem each side; length: 53½ inches. Pattern was
stenciled on already prepared curtain as there is no stenciling on reverse side of hem.
Colors: red, indigo, and green.

    Curtain comes from East Lexington, Massachusetts and dates from 1775–1800 or
possibly earlier. It was prepared for a specific window in the Stephens Robbins House
(a saltbox built circa 1750) and set aside to await stenciler in neighborhood.—Photograph
courtesy The Society for the Preservation of New England Antiquities, Boston

A single window curtain, woven of single-ply linen with unusual vertical multistripe.
Alternating vegetable-dyed colors of rosy red and gold with indigo in a pattern repeat
on otherwise plain ground. The stripes are set in the warp threads; the indigo partial
stripe design was made either by dipping a hank of linen into the dye pot before
preparing the warp or was "painted" on with dye after warping and before weaving.
The same ⅛-inch twill tape as was shown in the preceding photograph is sewn into
the top heading, spaced about 4½ inches apart. The turned heading of approximately
3 inches is left free with its own ⅜-inch hem. The bottom hem of the curtain is
⅛ inch, the width 30¾ inches with selvedges only, and the length 53½ inches. Weft
yarn is single-ply linen, undyed.

    Curtain dates circa 1800 and comes from the same house as did the curtain
shown in the preceding photograph.—Photograph courtesy The Society for the
Preservation of New England Antiquities, Boston

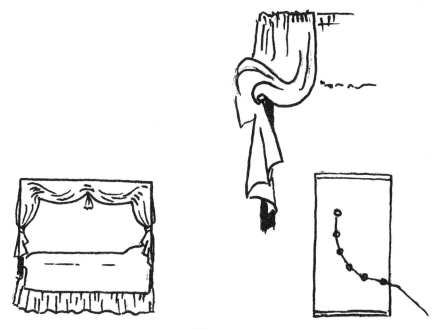

FESTOONS

Left: *Four-post bed with festoons made by shirring at three points, creating a draped effect. Purely decorative with valance and curtain now combined, these were most likely seen in better rural bed chambers.* Right: *Festooned bed curtain. The festoon effect was achieved by rings and a cord pull sewn to back of curtain. The cord may have been fastened to a small knob on the bed post. This would probably not have been seen. The heading and valance were gathered and perhaps tacked to the tester.*

rail, or bottom of the headboard. The two side curtains and two foot curtains could be pulled together to completely enclose the bed from light and protect it from cold drafts. From the seventeenth to the mideighteenth century the foot panels went outside and over the foot posts, drawing to meet at the center foot of the bed. They also were drawn to meet the side panels midway on the sides of the bed. The side panels hung on each side of the head end of the bed and also could be drawn to the centers of the sides, meeting the foot end curtains.

The bed curtains were pulled together by means of small brass rings, approximately one inch in diameter, attached to ⅜-inch tape which was in turn sewn to the curtains. These were fairly regularly spaced at intervals anywhere from four to ten inches apart, depending on the weight of the fabric and width of curtain. Loops of woven tape were also used in place of rings. The tape was often hand-loomed on a small tape loom, and woven with linen in twill approximately ⅜ inch wide. A doubled tape loop about two inches long (from top of curtain to top of folded loop) was common, although some measured as long as three inches.

The curtains, when pulled, slid along wooden or iron rods attached to the post just below the frame of the tester. Wooden rods were thought to have had a screw eye in the end of the rod. Each rod had a fairly sturdy diameter of approximately ¾ inch. The screw eyes went over pintles in the post, securing the rod. There may also have been cords through loops or rings to aid in pulling. However, this is only conjecture, and there were undoubtedly improvisations, such as hooks or nails for rods.

The side head curtains measured from thirty to thirty-five inches in width. Covering about twice the area of the side curtain, the foot curtains were almost double in width, sixty to seventy inches. Sometimes they were considerably more than double width. The movable

FOUR-POST BED VALANCE CUT
TO SIMULATE FESTOONS

Here head cloth, valance, and flounce are of matching plaid. The flounce is smooth, not gathered. However, the gathered flounce continued to be used during the nineteenth century and sometimes became part of the spread itself.

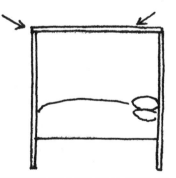

TESTER FRAME FOR GREAT
BED AND FOUR-POST BED

Top: *View from above.* Bottom: *As it sits atop four posts of bed.*

*Bed hanging, in medium blue and white furniture check pattern, woven of single-ply linen. Checks measure 1⅝ inches by 1¾ inches. The ⅜-inch casing for the drawstring is hand-sewn with a running stitch, with flounce approximately 2¼ inches deep. All sides are sewn with a ¼-inch linen binding. Bed curtain is one of a set (not necessarily complete) of three curtains, two very wide and one narrow. The panels are woven in a 30-31-inch width, two of which are sewn together for larger curtains. The length of the curtains is longer than the usual tester length, suggesting they may have been hung by drawstrings somehow from overhead beams. These curtains possibly were used to surround a low bed or folding bed. Judging from the width of the panels, they were probably homewoven. This eighteenth-century hanging was found in Rockville, Connecticut.—*Photograph courtesy The Society for the Preservation of New England Antiquities, Boston

curtains hung from the tester just to the floor, the measurement governed by the height of the tester. Curtains were finished with narrow hems approximately ⅛ inch wide. The foot curtains were often omitted entirely by the end of the eighteenth century in the wealthier homes. However, in the remote farming areas the seventeenth-century custom of sleeping on the first floor with the family members' beds in various rooms was carried on with the traditional bed furnishings used long after the Revolution. The parents usually slept in the parlor in the great bed with its bed furniture in the seventeenth and into the eigh-

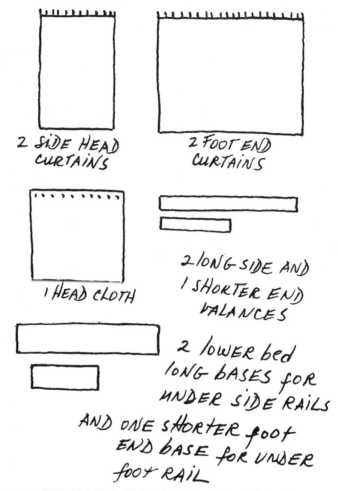

BED HANGINGS FOR EIGHTEENTH-CENTURY GREAT BED

teenth century. By the late eighteenth century the bed chamber became a room separate from the parlor, usually off the kitchen. In many rural households the tradition of parents sleeping on the first floor continued, with older children in loft or garret, and by the late nineteenth century, generally, the full set of bed hangings gave way to bed without tester.

The half-headed bedstead, with curtains and valance, was a folding bed that required the closing of concealing curtains when not in use. Standing free, it had two posts at either side of the headboard that were extended to the height of five to six feet; sometimes a separate frame was attached to the wall. Built onto the posts and at a right angle to them

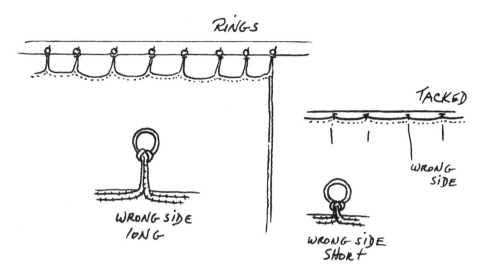

TWO WAYS OF HANGING HEADCLOTH

Stationary bed hangings such as headcloth were sometimes hung by tape looped around rings, with the tape then sewn to top of curtain. The rings hung over hooks or nails on the tester frame. The length of the tape from the rings down to the hem varied from 1 to 2½ inches. Sometimes the headcloth was merely tacked to the frame and eased slightly, and sometimes tape loops, without rings, were used.

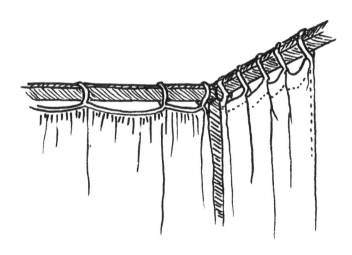

GATHERED HEADCLOTH

In the nineteenth century the headcloth was often gathered onto tape and bound with loops, or sometimes tapes, for tying. The side head curtain also hung by loops. It was no longer wide for protection, but simply decorative.

was the overhanging valance frame, which held the valance and supported a rod or heavy wire for the curtains.

The curtains were sometimes pulled along an iron rod, secured inside the overhead wooden valance frame. Each curtain was either suspended from rings, approximately five to six inches apart, around which narrow tape was looped and sewn to the top inside of the curtain; or instead of rings, the curtain top was sewn with a ⅜–½-inch casing which gathered on a bent rod on the outside of the valance frame, allowing the curtain to be pulled. The curtains met at center foot, in either case. The head cloth hanging against the wall end of the bed may have been tacked to the tester frame or hung by a cord through the casing, and tied to nails.

The valance may have been tacked on, by a heading, or tied on after having been gathered or tucked onto a narrow heading, and ties sewn on at intervals for securing to the frame. Since this was a lesser bed, it might have had a featherbed, but possibly it simply had a bed-tick filled with straw. The blankets and bed cover would be home-woven wool, dyed and woven in bright checks or plaids. Sometimes the bed curtains were checks, and the blankets rough and plain or plaid, sufficing for cover or spread over the nonconforming mound of feather-bed. These beds were charming in their fresh colors and naive simplicity.

The *press bed*, or *closet bed*, was essentially the same as the half-headed bedstead, but without the half-headed frame, and derived its name

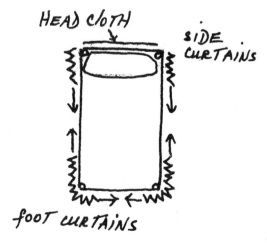

EIGHTEENTH-CENTURY
BED CURTAINS ON GREAT
BED, SHOWING POSITIONS
AND DRAWING DIRECTONS

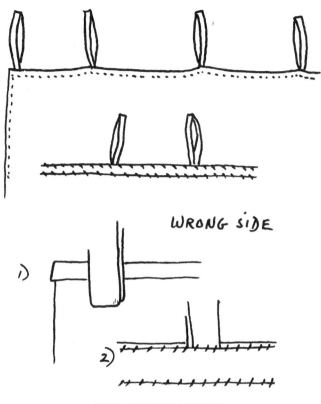

BED CURTAIN LOOPS

Bed curtains, hanging from iron or wooden rods fastened to tester frame, were drawn along the rods by curtain loops. Sewn with tape or self-fabric, the loops were made approximately ⅜ inch wide and varied in length from 1½ to 3 inches long, doubled. Generally about 2 inches long and spaced at 5-6-inch intervals, the loops were sewn on back of curtain (see 1). Tape or self-fabric loops were also used as facing, sewn over the loop ends to conceal them (see 2).

from being folded into a closet made especially for the purpose. The featherbed or ticking was folded right in when the bed was upended. Sufficient evidence has not been established as to whether the bedding was strapped in. It may have simply been held with the hand while upending and stayed in place once pressed in. The press bed was pressed into the closet when not in use, and when the closet doors closed, it appeared to be a paneled cupboard. Inside the closet were hooks that held the bed in place, securing it to the wall. Sometimes the free headboard of the bed was implanted in the plaster of the inside closet at the proper level and the

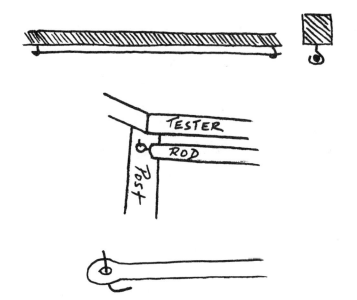

THREE WAYS OF HANGING RODS

Top: Rod supported by hooks. Center: *Rod with screw eye-type fastening.* Bottom: *Rod secured by a hole in its end around a naillike hook.*

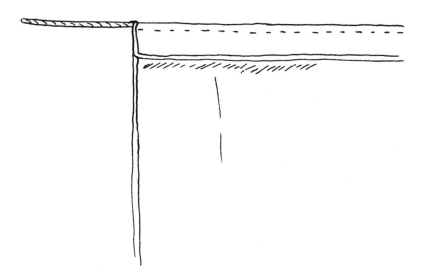

SIMPLE ARRANGEMENT FOR HANGING BED CURTAIN

Casing for drawstring stitched at the top. The edges are hemmed with a ⅜-inch turn or bound.

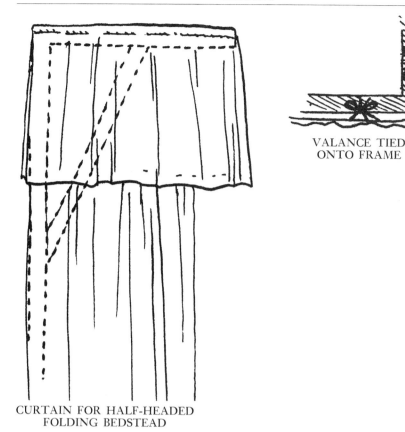

VALANCE TIED
ONTO FRAME

CURTAIN FOR HALF-HEADED
FOLDING BEDSTEAD

bed frame was simply hooked on. The bed furnishings would have been simple bed-ticking, sheeting, and blankets.

FABRICS USED FOR RURAL BED HANGINGS

Although there is little seventeenth-century linsey-woolsey in existence, inventories furnish documentary evidence of its use as early as 1649 in Wenham, Massachusetts. Later records document its use in colors such as blue, brown, and green, and natural white was also thought to have been used. Linsey-woolsey was usually woven of fine single-ply linen in plain weave. Very fine plain white linen was also used, and for lesser beds, rough-spun coarse woolen in plain weave. Sometimes linens were woven of fine twill for bed curtains. These fabrics continued in use into the late nineteenth and even the early twentieth century. Some hand-woven dimity—a white corded material woven of varying weights of cotton to achieve the rib effect—has been found, but dimity was not commonly homemade. In the late eighteenth and early nineteenth centuries, fringes, usually 1½–2 inches, either purchased or made on the tape loom at home, were added to the vertical edges of curtains and lower edges of valances of home-woven linen to "update" them.

Furniture checks, often of the ⅞-inch size, were common for valance and bed hangings. The wide use of furniture check is documented in *The Farmer's Friend, or the History of Mr. Charles Worthy* (Boston, 1793). The author, Enos Hitchcock, writes that the farmhouse "parlour chamber [the bedroom over the parlor] was made the stile of the parlour [which had furniture check window curtains in red and white], with the addition of a bed of furniture check."

The Copp family textile collection at the Smithsonian has a complete set of furniture check blue and white bed hangings, including a valance lined with buckram, curtains with head cloth, and an unlined counterpane that hangs almost to the floor. Along with the set there are four pair of window curtains, all woven of single-ply linen in plain weave. These date from the late eighteenth century. The valance is fifteen inches with slightly gathered fullness. Another set of bed hangings from the Copp family, thought to be late eighteenth-century, has a valance and three bed curtains of plain weave white linen with linen tape loops. The white valance is 16½ inches deep.

THE VALANCE

The *tester* was a wooden frame joining the tops of the bed posts. It was covered with a *tester cloth*, which was stretched over the open frame, forming a tent effect over the bed. The *valance* (also spelled "valans" or "valins") was most often made of the same cloth as the curtains and lined with a stiff fabric such as buckram, or even paper. During the seventeenth and eighteenth centuries the valance was commonly made approximately twelve inches deep, with a narrow ⅛-inch hem. Three separate pieces were made to cover the upper part of the tester sides and foot end. These were hand-stitched together. Sometimes contrasting braid, binding, or fringe was used for trim by the wealthy. Fringe, although documented as early as the seventeenth century, was not in common use until the nineteenth century. In the rural areas until the midnineteenth century little trim was available, and edgings were sim-

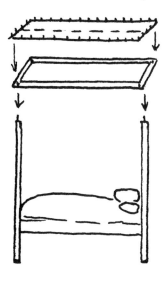

TESTER AND TESTER CLOTH

The tester cloth, made of two or three panels sewn together, was tacked onto the top of the tester. The tester frame, made to fit the bed exactly, was held in place by nails at tops of bed posts. Valance was then attached to tester frame.

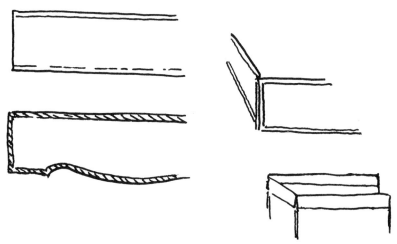

THE VALANCE

Top left: *Early eighteenth-century valance, plain with buckram backing and hemmed.* Bottom left: *Slightly shaped with trim of binding such as twill tape.* Top right: *Corner view.* Bottom right: *Complete three-piece valance in place.*

135

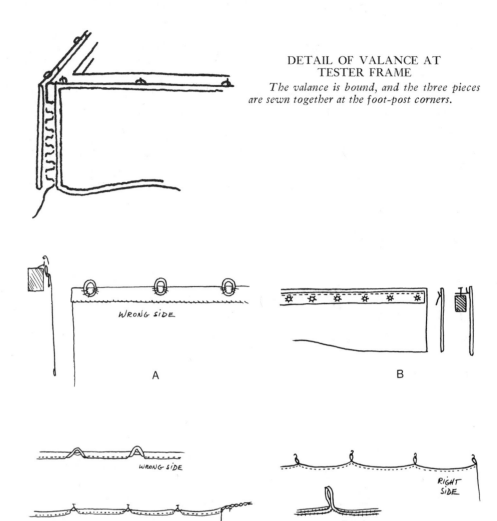

DETAIL OF VALANCE AT TESTER FRAME

The valance is bound, and the three pieces are sewn together at the foot-post corners.

A

B

C

D

METHODS OF HANGING VALANCE

A. *Valance hung by rings.* Left: *Valance in profile, showing cross-section of frame, nail, ring, and valance as it might have hung from nail.* Right: *Wrong side of valance in detail, showing rings sewn onto hem.* B. *Valance fastened to tester frame by means of nails through eyelets.* Left: *Wrong side of valance, with facing sewn at top. Lower part of facing with eyelet holes is free.* Center: *Profile of valance, with lower part of facing hanging free.* Right: *Facing hung onto nails through eyelets, causing it to become perpendicular to valance.* C. *Valance hung by nails from tester frame, or even an overhead beam, using a cord drawn through casing with occasional openings for cord to hook over nail.* D. *Valance hung by sewn-on tapes from hooks or nails on tester or overhead beam.*

GATHERED VALANCE

During the late eighteenth and early nineteenth centuries the valance was sometimes gathered by a drawstring inside a folded casing, finely stitched at heading.

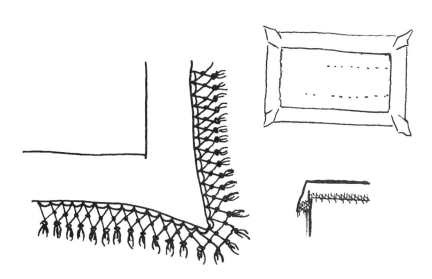

VALANCE OF THE EARLY NINETEENTH CENTURY

Left: *Elongated corner as it fell in point from valance frame. The hand-tied fringe shown was popular and was also used on bed curtains and straight window curtains.* Top right: *Overall view from above, showing valance and tester cloth sewn together as one piece.* Bottom right: *Valance as it hung over bedpost.*

ply neatly turned narrow hems. It is supposed that the valance top was attached to the tester by some means such as tacks or hooks, but there is little documented evidence to go on. It is also thought that possibly tapes or rings were sewn onto the valance top, and it hung from the tester by hooks; even a cord drawn through a casing at the valance top may have been caught by tacks or hooks. About 1800 the valance was made with a narrow half-inch to one-inch casing handstitched at the top fold of the heading, and a cord or tape was run through the casing to draw the valance in slight gathers. The inside heading remained free, but was hemmed or bound with a quarter-inch turn or binding. This free inside ruffle gave body to the valance top and may have also provided a means of tacking the gathers to the tester. The valance at this time and into the nineteenth century was lengthened to approximately 20 inches.

BASE AND FLOUNCE

Bases were listed with the bed furnishings, most frequently in seventeenth-century and early eighteenth-century inventories. The base was the fabric that hung from the two side and single foot rails of the early eighteenth-century bed to the floor. It was not what is now termed a twentieth-century dust ruffle, but was a plain, flat, and unshirred piece of material, usually of the same fabric as the bed curtains.

The flat base used on the seventeenth-century and early eighteenth-century bed consisted of three pieces, one for each side and the end of the bed. It was made approximately 20 inches deep, depending on the measurement from the supporting rod on the rail to the floor. The rod was thought to have been attached to the inside of the bed rail by some device such as nail, hook, or fixture.

In the mid- to late eighteenth century some bases were eliminated, along with foot end curtains, exposing both floor and end posts. Later in the eighteenth century (after 1789) the base became part of the outer layer of the coverlet, being an extended side of the quilted coverlet or counterpane. In the nineteenth century the gathered flounce was popular, with material slightly tucked or shirred into a narrow heading. Tapes

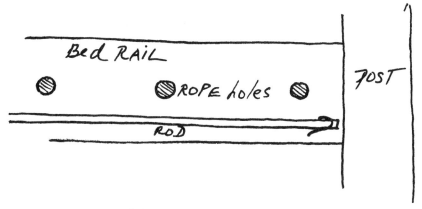

ROD FOR HANGING BASE

It may have been attached to the bed rail by means of a hook or bent nail. The base hung inside the rail below the ropes.

sewn at intervals onto the heading were used to tie the flounce onto the rods inserted inside the bed rail. In some cases the flounce was tied around the bed posts at the height of the top of the bed rail, creating a continuous flounce on sides, end, and corners. The coverlet hung eight to ten or more inches over the rail, covering the top of the flounce completely. In the late nineteenth century the flounce became part of the counterpane and

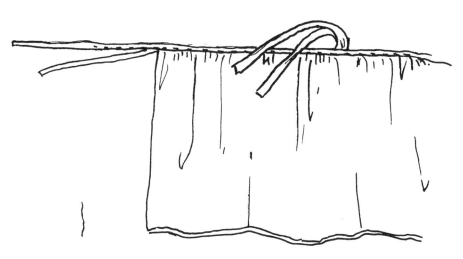

GATHERED FLOUNCE

The flounce was bound with tape or heading of fabric and shirred with the tape or fabric sewn over. The tape or fabric heading was tied to hook or nail inside rail.

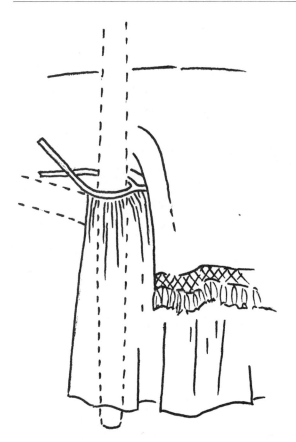

MIDNINETEENTH-CENTURY FLOUNCE

The flounce was tied over bed-posts at the foot end as well as at the sides. On fancier beds the flounce had fringe as well as the valance and matching window curtains.

was shirred on at the top of the side, falling almost to the floor. The gathered flounce continued in popularity into the twentieth century.

Decorated Bed Furnishings

The yearning for bright color was ever present, quite contrary to the belief that colonial days were drab days. The need and desire to express design in her own colorful way was a rewarding challenge to the country wife as well as her wealthy city sister. By the mideighteenth century life had become more secure so that when time would allow, she decorated her own bed furnishings with highly individualized charm. At first she had to spin and dye her own embroidery yarns.

Bed flounce hung from inside bed rail to floor by ties. Woven of blue and white single-ply linen, plain weave. Slightly tucked and irregular gathering sewn into band of finely checked blue and white linen. Hand-woven tape of blue and white for tying sewn onto band. Dimensions are 17½ inches by 117 inches. The flounce dates from the late eighteenth century and was found in the vicinity of Cheshire, Connecticut.—Old Sturbridge Village photograph by Donald F. Eaton

For deep yellows she yellowed further the tag-locks from the sheep by leaving them in the sun. She dipped the same yellowed tag-locks in the indigo pot for a very permanent blue-green. Then she had the madder reds to use, and logwood and nut browns, and shades of true blue from indigo. Later, if she could afford them, English crewel (worsted) yarns and patterns and cochineal red dyes were available in the cities or from the peddlers. Embroidery was taught mother to daughter. The learning slate was the sampler, country girl or not. Embroidery was considered such a necessary womanly art that needlework schooling was part of the wealthy girl's education. Boston had such a boarding school as early as 1714.

New England women created their early embroidery with a sense of freedom and delight, refreshing in its naïveté and openness. It was designed with a lighter, freer hand than the English, far removed from the heavy, somber eastern feel of the Jacobean English style favored by the wealthy in the seventeenth century. Hardly more than twelve stitches were used; the most popular were the self-couching stitches known as the Roumanian, New England economy, or laid stitch; the running stitch, buttonhole stitch, and outline. Yarns were precious and had to go far. The laid stitch was among the most economical, for the yarn was worked so that most of it lay on top of the cloth with only a bare outline showing on the reverse or wrong side. Instead of the closely worked acanthus leaves, thick vines, and other large motifs of English embroidery the New England housewife selected subjects surrounding her in her daily life—the flowers, trees, and animals. Floral designs were created with thin airy lines in brilliant colorings, sometimes incorporating ancestral symbols such as the Tudor rose, Irish trefoil, Scottish thistle, or tulips. Several kinds of flowers sprang from one root. Birds, deer, squirrels, and fruit trees made beguiling subjects. Eventually an art form evolved, truly American, no longer English.

Discussed here are those items embroidered on handwoven textiles.

BED HANGINGS

Bed hangings and valances were logical items to adorn. The bed and its furnishings remained the highest-valued possession in the household for decades. Often the coverlet or counterpane and head cloth were designed to match. Usually these bed furnishings were woven of linen and bleached white (though most of the existing ones have mellowed with age to a creamy golden color) in a fine plain or twill weave; some have been found to have counterpane tops of diaper weave.

The valance shown from the collection of the Museum of Fine Arts in Boston was embroidered on fine plain weave linen with squirrels, deer, and butterflies. It shows the breaking away from the English design influence in its more open spacing. However, the deer and exotic birds seem to retain their English heritage. Dated 1714, it was worked primarily in Roumanian stitch, and its colors are brilliant today.

Close-up of crewel work valance, dated 1714. Homespun linen ground, worked in reds, golds, greens, and brown, primarily in Roumanian stitch.—Photograph courtesy Museum of Fine Arts, Boston

Bed valance (same as that shown in preceding close-up). Delightful with carnation blowing in breeze, butterflies, dog, deer, rabbits, exotic birds, and a variety of trees. Note unusual house beyond hill. Worked on homespun linen.—Photograph courtesy Museum of Fine Arts, Boston

A rare example of an existing complete set of bed hangings beautifully embroidered and still vibrant in its coloring today is the work of Mary Bulman of York, Maine. The set was worked on homespun linen, now mellowed with age. It was made circa 1745 and is complete with side and foot hangings, head cloth, valance, and counterpane, all exquisitely embroidered in astonishingly balanced style, yet with the openness of design so typically American.

QUILTED COVERLETS

Although these are discussed in the coverlet section, they are mentioned here because they were often made of homespun, home-woven woolen which was dyed, glazed with an egg white mixture, and quilted with linen thread using a lamb's-wool filler and rougher woven home spun backing, usually of a different color. These appear frequently in eighteenth-century inventories.

An interesting pieced wool quilt is illustrated on page 121. It was made of cut pieces of handwoven woolen cloth of various colors which were sewn together, filled, and backed. Dating from the early nineteenth century, it is in the Old Sturbridge Village collection. Other pieced all-wool quilts sometimes had alternating sections embroidered.

Early in the nineteenth century white on beds was very much in vogue and many of the affluent homes' bedrooms were dressed in white cotton dimity or other "new" cotton fabrics. One of the quilting forms that became part of the white fashion for beds was *trapunto*, also known as *white work* or *stuffed work*. It required a fine pure white top material, and a backing of coarser homespun linen. The quilting design was more of a relief effect with raised vines and floral sprays, plump pineapples, and grapes with fine background stitching. The raised effect was created by poking cotton into the already stitched to-be-raised area from the coarser backing material. In fact, the home-woven backing was almost a necessity even when imported or fine cotton was used as the top layer.

Although trapunto was thought to be more the pastime of city women and in particular a southern art, a completely home-woven example of a comparatively plain design is in the Essex Institute, Salem, Massachusetts. It has an interesting history. A handwritten note of 1880 by Mary R. Crownenshield says the spread was made by her great-great-grandmother, Mary Crownenshield. The top is of extremely fine handwoven linen, she writes, "being spun and woven by her—and put out to bleach on the 19th of May 1780—the day known as the dark day" (perhaps an eclipse that day?). It seems fair to assume that the woven linen topping was incorporated in the spread at a later date, along with the coarser backing linen, which was woven of linen tow fibers and has a mixed tannish gray appearance. Evidence of the cotton stuffing is visible from the tufts exposed at points where it was poked in. The overall design is simple and graceful. Large areas of the background are left plain with no quilting other than the outlining of the design motif itself.

COUNTERPANES

Several handwoven fabrics were used with differing effects as counterpanes. Linen counterpanes of fine plain, twill, or diaper weave were embroidered to match a valance or bed hangings. Single-ply wool woven in a twill was used for counterpanes in white, and also dyed very dark black and indigo. The dark wool twills were embroidered with light bright colors creating very dramatic effects with central floral sprays and borders. They were usually woven in two panels, seamed vertically.

EMBROIDERED WOOL BLANKETS

These blankets, woven of natural white wool in plain weave or twill, were thought to be used as "show" blankets in warmer weather when woven coverlets were set aside. Woven in two panels seamed vertically, they were embroidered with relatively crude yarn and long stitches in large eight- to ten-inch sunbursts and rose-point compasses of reds, oranges, and yellows in the corners. Sometimes they were a little more elaborate with reverse curve borders and smaller motifs interpersed as well.

WINDOWPANE CHECK BLANKETS

These were still another embroidered counterpane creation in the late eighteenth and early nineteenth centuries. Each blanket was first woven with the indigo crosslines forming open three- to four-inch squares. Then bird and floral motifs were embroidered in the center of each block with bright colors, or shades of blue. Sometimes a vine or leaf design was embroidered along the outermost squares as a border. These blankets were woven in two or three panels, seamed vertically.

SPREADS

Although the *stenciled spreads* were usually made of a fine, plain, inexpensive purchased cotton, there have been examples of stenciling worked on fine homespun linen. Stenciling was popular over a period of thirty to forty years beginning in 1820. One stencil was cut for each color from oiled paper. The colors were painted through the stencil with a tampon, one color at a time. The paint pigment in oil was made permanent by mixing with a stencil mordant. The resulting designs were crisp and simple, and repeat motifs were planned to achieve a colorful and pleasing summer counterpane.

A tufted bedspread, now the property of the Wenham Museum, Massachusetts, was handmade by Julia A. Berry Cutterson of Brookline, Massachusetts circa 1830. It is of handwoven white cotton, possibly itinerant-made, with handtufting and handfringing. Woven of two 41½-

inch panels seamed vertically, each edge is fastidiously turned ⅛ inch, the 6½-inch fringe applied, and a ⅛- to ³⁄₁₆-inch facing sewn in minute stitches. The body of the spread is covered overall with multiple-strand tufts one inch long, sewn through the single-layer spread three inches apart. The fringe is 6½ inches deep, with 4 knotted rows, and is made of 4-ply cotton twine, factory-spun.

chapter 5

WINDOW CURTAINS

Architectural Changes, 1620–1850

CURTAINS USED IN the rural American farmhouse have an interesting history from their strange nonexistence in the seventeenth and early eighteenth centuries to their many beguiling country adaptations of the wealthy imported fashions dating 1750–1850. The use of curtains, or lack of them, was governed in part by the architectural forms of these houses. Curtain styles changed several years after architectural changes occurred, and in rural areas fashion was ever slow to arrive.

The very earliest dwellings in New England at Plimouth Plantation, Plymouth, Massachusetts, are thought to have been of the four post-hole, wattle-and-daub construction, with a wood-framed chimney

148

and thatched roof. They were basically a one-room, dirt or plank floor home, with sleeping area slightly separated. The window allotment was one to a room—one in the main area and one in the sleeping area. They can hardly be thought of as windows in the twentieth-century concept. The houses were built to keep the inhabitants as warm as their familiar homeland traditions of homebuilding knowledge allowed. The need for privacy and ventilation had not been established. The colonists were accustomed to sleeping three and four people to a bed—adults, children, and animals living in the same confined area. The need for protection from the cold, the "bad night air," and rodents was greater. Therefore, the settlers' windows were minuscule by our standards. Approximately eight inches square, each window had two narrow vertical bars and was covered with oiled paper. Bear grease was considered the best oil and gave the paper a slightly translucent quality. In the surrounding structural framing of the window were grooves for a sliding wood panel to completely cover the window inside the house. This was hardly a house for the finer dignities of living. It was simply a house to shelter and protect the family and animals. There were crops to start, mouths to feed, and hopes of survival and better days to come.

Although none remain standing, these very early houses of the 1630s were thought to have been numerous. Their simplicity made them easily erected, allowing the tasks of raising food and hunting to assume a new priority. But the first severe winters soon made it evident that there must be changes in the house construction. Wood was added for siding, stronger, more hardy timber framing was needed, and eventually larger windows. The windows still remained small, but considerably larger than the eight-inch square of the earliest homes. The casement of small leaded panes evolved, with sliding panel for opening—a testimony to the lasting Elizabethan influence.

The fireplaces became brick, laid in the Elizabethan manner, and the single room of early times became more like the "great hall" of English houses. In a single-room home, cooking, eating, and sleeping still took place there, with separate quarters for the animals. In a two-room house with central chimney, the cooking and eating took place in the "kitchen," and the other room, called the "great hall," was the living room, or parlor, with its "great bed" for sleeping. The Parson

SEVENTEENTH-CENTURY WINDOW
AT PLIMOUTH PLANTATION

The grooves in the upper beam and the cross-piece beneath the window were for a sliding wood panel which covered the inside of the window. The window was eight inches square and covered with oiled paper.

SEVENTEENTH-CENTURY
CASEMENT WINDOW OF
SMALL LEADED PANES

A sliding panel on one side opened horizontally.

Capen House (1683) in Topsfield, Massachusetts, the Whipple House (1638) in Ipswich, Massachusetts, and the Hemsted House (1678) in New London, Connecticut are among fine examples still standing. The leaded, paned casement windows of this type house apparently were not curtained. Any reference to curtains in inventories of this early period was in the context of bed furnishings. Paintings of the period in Europe rarely show window curtains; usually the windows are pane casements. Sometimes, but rarely, a large, single heavy curtain can be seen draped to one side. However, this was used as a partition in a room, or for keeping out drafts in doorways. There is a great lack of evidence that curtains were used frequently at windows. Bed curtains *were* commonly used and it is these that we find in evidence in the wills and inventories.

The single-room house became the half-house with the addition of a second floor. When later the second large room on the first floor was added, the chimney became central. And still later, as the family grew, by opening and enlarging the chimney at rear, another room across the back of the house became the *keeping room*, or "kitchin"—a room for preparing and cooking food, eating, spinning, weaving, and even sleeping—a general workroom and gathering place. The front parlor and dining room became more special. When the parlor was first set aside for entertaining, curtains came into frequent use, but just for the parlor in rural areas. Leantos at the rear gave additional space for sheltering animals or perhaps a buttery or another bedroom, often called a borning room, where sick or otherwise confined people needing special care were close to the kitchen. This extended first floor and leanto evolved into the saltbox shape, allowing room for two bedchambers at the top of a staircase and space over the leanto. This form became commonly used for many decades in the rural areas. Many small farms retained the bedroom on the first floor, with parlor opposite and keeping room in the rear, with extensions added on for sheltering animals. This was a basic three-room house. Variations on the two-room Cape Cod cottage were also popular. Thus, the central chimney with the general layout of two to three large rooms surrounding persisted with its many variations. The saltbox and Cape Cod cottage both remain New England favorites today, with all their many ramifications and appendages. The early farmhouse with connecting sheds, shelters, and barns is unique to New England, and standing evidence of the New Englanders' ability to adapt to climate and need, while at the same time hanging onto the practicalities of tradition that made sense to the farmer's individual way of life.

The windows in these first colonial houses, in spite of variety in the house structure itself, were for the most part generally the same in rough dimensions. No longer leaded casements in the Elizabethan style, they became double-hung with multipaned glass. The glass was expensive and had to be imported at first. In these windows small panes were set in rows in wooden mullions, in combinations of twelve, nine, and six—such as twelve over twelve or nine over six. These combinations, in

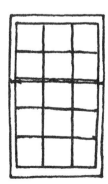

EIGHTEENTH-CENTURY HUNG SASH WINDOW
This window had six panes over nine panes and opened vertically. Such small-paned windows remaind in rural areas for generations.

turn, determined the overall dimensions of the windows. Generally, they were long and quite narrow, proportioned approximately two times as long as they were wide. In the cold North they were sparsely spaced, often with only one window per room, and usually two in a larger room. Farther south, where the climate was a little kinder, the windows were placed a little lower to the ground and were slightly wider.

Throughout the first colonial period to the middle of the eighteenth century, there is little evidence to confirm any common usage of curtains at the windows. Windows were mainly a source of light, and one kept away from their drafts in winter, gravitating to the fire and its light. Without some kind of central heating, the early houses were chilly. Evidence abounds to the fact—even to ink being kept in a shirt pocket, as otherwise the ink would freeze while one was writing. Obviously, windows were hardly to sit by during the cold months.

By the mideighteenth century, the architectural form changed. About 1750 it was fashionable among the wealthy to have a new home built with a central hall and staircase. Chimneys built into the outside walls of two opposite front rooms now assumed importance. In the homes of the wealthy, the windows became slightly wider and longer, and were treated on the interior in an architectural manner, thanks to the new craze for paneling. Raised paneled wainscoting, a paneling applied to the lower half of interior walls, structural features such as pilasters set in well-designed and carved fireplace paneling, and beautiful molding trim became important. Windows were an integral part of the whole room, fitted with raised paneled folding shutters or sliding "Indian shutters." Windows with the now slightly larger panes were not curtained. The paneled shutters "dressed" the windows, which for the first time took on significant interest as part of the total architectural design of the rooms.

The rural areas adopted the paneling vogue slowly, as with everything fashionable, for it was the wealthy near the seaport towns that were first to take to it. West of seaport towns, trees were just being felled for new houses and barns, whereas the sawmills near the shipbuilding industries were busy with lumber that would be used for paneling in the homes near the seaports. Shipbuilding carpenters, with their professional skill and adaptability, were readily available in the seaport towns to erect raised paneling for homes. A well-to-do country squire might be among the first in the village to have a carpenter make fine paneling in his relatively lavish country home. Farmhouses had paneling in time, to a lesser degree, but usually only on fireplace walls and perhaps in the parlor. However, curtains were another story; many inland farmhouse windows remained shutterless and curtainless for several generations beyond 1750. There is much folk art depicting family scenes, where surprisingly as late as the midnineteenth century there are still no curtains, but rather colorfully painted trim on window sashes and doors. Charles Dickens, writing about his first visit to America in 1842 in *American Notes*, describes some windows: "Those slightly-built wooden dwellings behind which the sun was setting with a brilliant lustre, could be looked through and through, that the idea of any inhabitant being able to hide himself from the public gaze, or to have any secrets from the public eye, was not entertainable for a moment. Even where a blazing fire shone through the uncurtained window of some distant house, it had the air of being newly lighted, and of lacking warmth. . . ."

Today there is a need for privacy and we have the desire to soften our windows, shield ourselves from the sun and cold, and to feed an esthetic desire for the color, design, and warmth of textiles at our windows and throughout our homes. We, too, have *our* adaptations and can take from our heritage that which seems fitting and works for us.

Early Window Curtains

Window curtains were first used in a rather haphazard way; sometimes a curtain was just one panel barely wide enough to cover the window, and pushed to the side when not needed to cover. This is substantiated in inventories listing odd numbers of window curtains. There is also evidence that the single panel was caught to one side by

LATE EIGHTEENTH-CENTURY WINDOW CURTAINS

Left: *Unshirred curtain, just hung on a string between two nails. Such curtains were often hung in lesser rooms such as butteries to shield from sun and cold.* Center: *Straight curtain casually tossed over peg to let in air and light.* Right: *Two panels with string running through narrow casing fastened around nails.*

means of a wooden peg on the window frame, slightly higher than half-way.

Supports for the earliest window curtains were of varying sophistication: anything from a linen string fastened at each end with a small nail or a whittled wooden rod resting on large flat-headed nails to wooden brackets cupped to hold the rod, with nails firmly securing the bracket top and bottom (a later development).

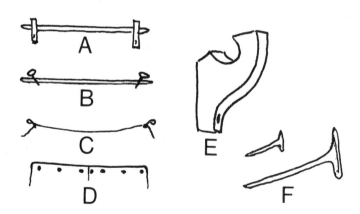

SUPPORTS FOR EARLY WINDOW CURTAINS

A. *Rod resting in wooden brackets.* B. *Whittled wooden rod resting on large flat-headed nails.* C. *String around nails.* D. *Tacks or nails.* E. *Close-up of wooden bracket.* F. *Close-up of flat-headed nails.*

Window curtains became commonly used and listed in inventories about the time of the Revolution and began to appear more frequently in pairs from then on. These were made with narrow loops at the headings. They were not full, but narrow panels just covering the window when pulled together. The tab at center window of each panel was ingeniously designed by being lengthened slightly on the inside facing. This enabled the curtain to hang straight, opened or closed. The loops varied from two to three inches in length and were sewn onto the curtaintop with facing over on the reverse side.

The curtains had narrow ¼-inch hems at the sides and approximately 2-inch hems at the bottom. In spite of other styles coming and going, these straight-hanging loop styles were popular for decades, and found as late as the nineteenth century in some rural areas. They were easy to make and launder, and took little material. In some rural areas windows remained curtainless except for the parlor into the nineteenth century. The frugal New England farmwife of that time may have considered window curtains impractical. Perhaps because of dirt, dust, flies, small children, and the lack of time, she couldn't care for and replace them.

The fabrics most frequently used were linsey-woolsey and, for the parlor, linen bleached as white as possible. If the farmwife had some-

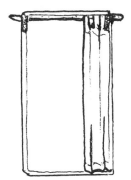

HALF-CURTAIN, PUSHED TO ONE SIDE

This curtain barely covered the window when closed.

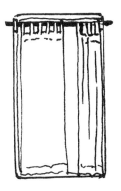

LOOP CURTAINS

These curtains with self-made loops hung straight from a wooden rod supported by nails or wooden brackets. This curtain style was in use from the late eighteenth to the late nineteenth century.

155

thing extra to barter with the Yankee peddler, she might choose a yard or two of a calico print from his wagon.

Window curtains in rural areas were used first in the parlor. This was considered the special room of the house, where the family would entertain visitors. The small-paned windows were curtained with finely woven homespun linen hung in narrow panels from tabs on a simple wooden rod. The linen had been washed and bleached snowy white by repeated laundering, then drying flat in the sunshine outside. Gradually, window curtains began to be used in the bedrooms or bed chambers, although the practice did not become universal. After the fashionable paneling craze of the wealthy, current about 1750, in the seaport towns, where paneled and painted shutters were used, the rural areas adapted the use of paint on window sashes as part of room decor. They also painted doors and modest paneling, but curtains, in some areas, were omitted. Later, in the 1850s, when stenciled walls, painted woodwork simulating wood grains, and fancy painted furniture were in vogue, we find a lack of curtains still in the farming areas. In other words, for a period of over 100 years (1750–1850), when wealthy people had beautiful brocades, prints and toiles from Europe, and fine American-made prints, there were *some* remote rural areas where window curtains were used only in a very limited way. Villages closer to the seaport towns such as Boston, Salem, and Newburyport understandably received more influence, and farmhouse windows there were hung with curtains in parlors and the more important bed chambers.

Window Curtains in the Late Eighteenth and Early Nineteenth Centuries

Curtains in this later period were fashioned in a number of ways. Sometimes they were made of two panels gathered by means of a narrow ½-inch or less casing at the top, threaded onto a string which was simply hung by nails on each side near the top of the window frame. A style used by the Copp family, whose homemade textiles are in the collections of the Smithsonian Institution, was made for four windows. Two panels for each window were stitched together at the top for a length of about 14 inches; each panel was about 24 inches wide, and the bottom

Close-up of furniture check linen spread, woven of single-ply linen in medium blue and white ½-inch check. Two edges have a rolled hem; the other two are selvedges. The spread dates from the early nineteenth century and comes from Warwick, Rhode Island.—Old Sturbridge Village photograph by Donald F. Eaton

Warp-faced striped carpet, woven on a home loom circa 1810–1850, from Auburn, Massachusetts. Top: *total view. Carpet has stripes of red, rose, gray, white, brown, tan, yellow, and orange. The warp is of dyed two-ply wool, cotton, and jute; the weft is brown factory-spun cotton.* Bottom: *close-up. Worn area shows brown weft cotton.*—Old Sturbridge Village photograph by Donald F. Eaton

Rag rug from Exeter, New Hampshire. Top: *total view.* Bottom: *close-up. Colors are blue, rose, green, yellow, black, tan, and brown. The warp yarns are factory-spun brown cotton; the filler is part dyed cotton fabric strips and part heavy wool yarn, woven in a planned pattern that simulates warp-faced stripe. Dimensions are 51 by 29 inches.*—Old Sturbridge Village photograph by Donald F. Eaton

Bed chamber off the kitchen in the Pliny Freeman Farmhouse as it appeared circa 1830. The cannonball bed is covered with a handwoven coverlet of indigo wool with cotton fringe of the period. Under bed is trundle bed of earlier period. Chair is child's barrel chair slipcovered with handwoven blue-and-white checked linen.—Old Sturbridge Village photograph by Donald F. Eaton hem was ⅛ inch. The top had a ¼-inch turn and 2-inch casing for cord or string. The curtain was probably tied back at the sides with cord tied to nails on each side of the window frame. These curtains were woven of blue and white furniture check, matching a set of bed hangings and counterpane (see the discussion of furniture check in the next chapter). Another technique for the same style was to tack the curtain material at the heading across the top of the window. Sometimes a valance of approximately ten inches was placed over the heading to hide the tacks. It was probably tacked from the flat edge of the window frame.

In the early to midnineteenth century the Empire style had its influence on window curtains as well as bed curtains. These were considered fashionable if matched in style; so along with the festoons and draping of the bed hangings, the window curtains had a more draped effect—caught in puffs with tiebacks of ribbon or tape tied on, hooked to the window side frame, sometimes at a considerably higher place. Sometimes a single panel was caught high to one side with tape. See the drawings for variations.

Handwoven fabrics used for curtains were linen in plain, striped, checked, and plaid patterns; linsey-woolsey; cotton and linen (in the

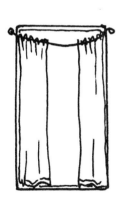

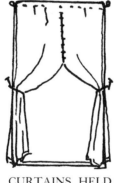

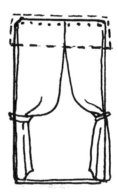

CURTAINS
SHIRRED BY
STRING
THROUGH
CASING

The string was tied to nails just below the top of the win-dow. Late eighteenth century.

CURTAINS HELD
BACK WITH
CORDS AND
NAILS

Casing for cord is about two inches at the top. Curtains have a narrow hem at bot-tom. Two panels are sewn together part-way (12-14 inches) down from top. Late eighteenth century.

FLAT PANELS
TACKED TO TOP
OF WINDOW
FRAME

These curtains were drawn to side with tiebacks and sometimes covered with valance to hide tacks. Late eighteenth century.

Fitch house parlor, of later period, with purchased wallpaper, upholstered Empire sofa, and Queen Anne tea table. Window curtains of fine purchased white-on-white cotton are shirred onto wooden rod and simply tied with bows of woven colored tapes. Note the eagle-stenciled rushbottom Hitchcock chairs. The wooden floor is painted with a diamond pattern. Window curtains date from circa 1820–1840.—Old Sturbridge Village photograph by Donald F. Eaton

nineteenth century), and home-woven fine linen stenciled or taken to a printer for tiny overall block-printing.

Fringes were home-woven for trim, and by the midnineteenth century some hand-tied netting was used for trim on bed and window alike.

One of the most popular window curtains over a prolonged period in rural areas was the tab-hung two-panel style. Directions are given below for sewing tab-hung curtains.

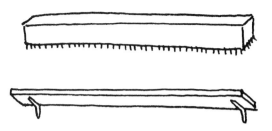

VALANCE AND SUPPORT

Top: *Valance seamed with box corner to fit over wood.* Bottom: *Wrought iron support holding wood valance support, about three inches deep, for window-top.*

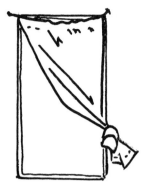

KNOTTED STYLE OF HANGING WINDOW CURTAIN

Curtain was knotted to one side to keep away from open window. This hanging method was used from the late eighteenth to the midnineteenth century. If there were two panels, each was knotted separately. The single-panel curtain shown was slightly gathered on string running through a narrow casing at top and fastened by nails.

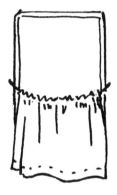

HALF-CURTAIN

In the nineteenth century a half-curtain was sometimes hung on the lower half of a window. It was gathered by string through a narrow casing and secured by nails on the frame.

CURTAIN ON WOODEN ROD SECURED BY WOODEN BRACKET

Curtain has tieback fastened high on frame one-fifth of the way down, narrow one-inch casing shirred on the rod, and a hem of about three inches.

CURTAINS TIED WITH BOWS

Each curtain has a casing of about two inches, a narrow side hem, and a bottom hem of about two inches. Curtains were tied about one-third of the way from the top.

SELF-LOOP CURTAINS

Curtains are supported by rod and bracket which are painted the color of the woodwork. The warm-weather style of hanging curtains is shown. String used to hold curtain up high is secured by nail slightly below top of window.

CURTAIN HUNG BY BRASS ROD WITH SMALL BALLS ON END

Curtain is draped in cascade and caught by knob.

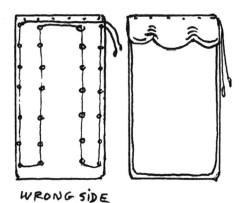

WRONG SIDE

DRAW CURTAIN

A single piece of fabric could cover the window or be pulled up as a draw curtain.

FRINGED CURTAIN AND VALANCE

Curtain is shirred onto rod. Note medallion for holding draped panel.

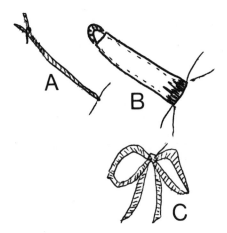

TIEBACKS

A. Cord or string fastened to nail. B. Strip of material, 12-14 inches long and 1½-2 inches wide, with fine hem and crocheted loop at end. C. Ribbon or tape tied in bow.

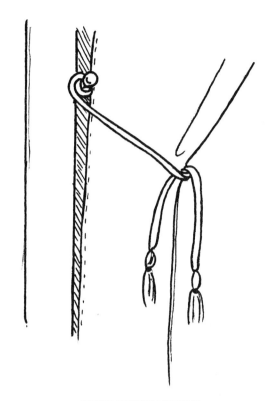

CORD WITH TASSEL

Cords with fringe or tassels were used in the midnineteenth century to hold back "fancy" curtains in bed chamber or parlor. Cords were kept in place by wooden knobs, painted the same color as the woodwork, protruding about half an inch from the window frame. Each cord was wound around knob at center of cord and then tied at curtain.

DIRECTIONS FOR MAKING TAB-HUNG
WINDOW CURTAINS

I. *Measuring*

A. *Length Measurement*

1. Measure from inside top to inside bottom (sill) of window.
2. To above measurement, add ¾ inch (for turn-down at top) and 2½ inches for hem and turned edge at bottom of panel. (Heavier material needs slightly more—⅛ inch.)

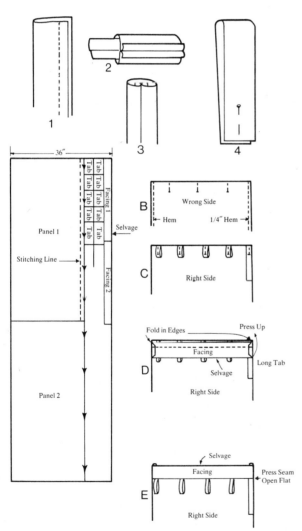

3. Total these measurements for cutting length of each panel (2 per window).

Note: If curtains are to hang covering the window frame and molding, add the width of sill and just *below* sill woodwork (or molding) to the above total.

B. *Width Measurement.* Early curtain panels were narrow and never a full 36-inch width. Measure inside molding across window plus 2 inches. Divide by 2 for width of each panel. Panels can be made an inch or two wider.

II. *Cutting.* Panels may be cut singly, lengthwise on material.

A. *Cutting Panels.* Remaining strip of material may be used for facings and tabs. See diagram.

1. Lay material flat on large oblong table or on floor.
2. With yardstick and soft lead pencil (which will wash out and is more exact than chalk marker), begin to mark each panel by marking across the width of material in 3-4 places. Then draw straight horizontal line with yardstick separating panel 1 from panel 2. Ideally this line should fall on or about the same weft thread across the fabric, as it is woven straight on the loom; however, it may be slightly distorted in washing and pressing. Do not, therefore, pull thread *across.* Panel 1.
3. Measure down length of panel desired amount. Mark across again and draw line for cutting Panel 2.
4. Measure width of panel, mark, and pull lengthwise thread at mark the length of panel, as shown by arrows in diagram.
5. Machine-stitch panel just ⅛ inch inside pulled thread before cutting lengthwise, so that panel will not stretch out of shape from handling.
6. Cut along pulled thread line and across panel but not into tab area.

B. *Cutting Tabs.* Tab lengths and widths vary, depending on thickness of material and placement of panel at window. A slightly larger allowance (⅛ inch) must be made for a rough, heavy woolen material, and the length of the tab seam must be trimmed after stitching the casing. A fine cotton or linen material is less bulky and does not need trimming. (*Note:* Measurements for tabs are given for curtains hanging *within* the casement of window. If curtain is to hang on rod placed on molding, above window, this distance should be measured from top of panel at top inside molding up over rod and down with 1½ inches allowance for sewing into panel.) Cut tabs on lengthwise grain of material (save selvage side strip for a neater finish for facing) approximately 2½ inches wide and 4½ inches long. Allow for 4 tabs of this length for each finished curtain and one additional (5 tabs in all per curtain panel) 2 inches longer, or 6½ inches long. This tab is placed at top side of panel that will fall at center of window. On the second panel of the pair, this tab position will be reversed. For one pair of curtains (2 panels) there are 10 tabs in all: 8 4½ inches long and 2 6½ inches long.

C. *Cutting Facing.* Using selvage, cut facings on lengthwise piece of material. There are two facing pieces per pair, one for each panel. The facings cross the panels horizontally on top. Cut each facing piece approximately 2½ inches deep and 1 inch wider than width of panel. The selvage edge of material will make a neat flat hem possible when hemming facing by hand.

◀II. Sewing
A. *Sewing Tabs.*
1. Tabs are stitched lengthwise on wrong side, with a ⅜-inch seam, and reversed like casing. See diagram.
2. Turn casing by forcing wrong side to inside. See diagram.
3. Press flat with flattened seam in center of tube. See diagram.
4. Fold to make loop; pin at unfinished end. See diagram.

B. *Sewing Panels.* Holding panel 1 lengthwise, pin a narrow ¼-inch turn (twice) on each side of panel, keeping on flat surface while turning and pinning. Sides should have previously been machine-stitched (see direction no. 5 under A. *Cutting Panels,* above). Press, avoiding pins. Hem by hand with fine overcast stitch. Remove pins; press flat again, using steam cloth. Repeat steps with panel 2. Bottom hems are best left unfinished until otherwise completed panels are hung at window 2-3 days, in case adjustment needs to be made. See diagram.

C. *Tabs.* With wrong side of hemmed panel placed down on flat surface, mark 5 places for tabs, 1 on each side, 3 in middle. Set 4 of 5 folded tabs *upside down* on top of panel. The fifth longer tab is pinned at *side* top of panel, but not folded. (The one free end is finished after facing is hemmed.) Pin and baste tabs firmly ½ inch down from top of panel. See diagram.

D. *Facing.* Still with wrong side of panel placed down on flat surface, place facing over (on top of) tabs, making sure that raw edges are placed at top of panel, with selvage edge of facing free to turn. Pin and baste top of panel, tabs, and facing together ½ inch from top edge, folding in facing edge even with panel edge and basting flat. Now machine-stitch ½ inch from edge. (This machine stitching does not show.) See diagram.

E. Press facing open as wide and sharp as you can. Use steam cloth if necessary. See diagram.

F. Fold facing down to wrong side, with tabs up. Press firmly again for a good sharp edge at top of panel. Pin; baste facing in place. Hand-hem with small stitches. Blindstitch at sides so that stitching won't show at edge. Turn in raw edge of long center tab about ¼ inch. Press; then hem 2 inches down at edge of facing. See diagram. (*Note:* Be sure that on second panel longer tab is in reversed position. The two longer tabs should be in center of window when curtains are hung.)

G. *Bottom Hem.* As a guide, the finished hem should measure 2 inches after ½-inch turn.

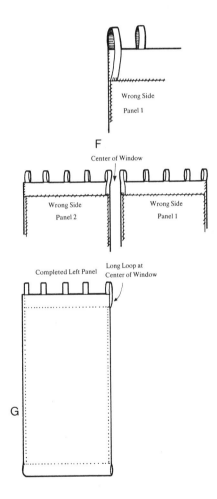

chapter 6

FURNITURE ACCESSORIES

Cushions

CUSHIONS—SPELLED QUYSHENS, cooshings, cushins, cussings, and other ways—were used for comfort in chairs that had rush, straw, or flag-woven bottoms. Traditionally black-painted chairs, such as the slat-back and bannister-back types, had colorful cushions. Stools were also cushioned. The seventeenth-century three-footed stools called *bofet* are thought to have had upholstered seats with the cushions built in. A probable rarity in rural areas, but nevertheless known to have existed in 1680 inventories of Massachusetts, was the cane chair with scroll carving on its high caned back. The seat of the chair, also caned, was cushioned. Another early caned chair, more like a chaise lounge because of its long

168

length, was called a *day bed*, or *couch*. This was cushioned with a long flat rectangular cushion, sometimes called a *squab*.

Cushions were fastened to chairs usually by means of ties or fabric self-loops. These loops were carried around the rear posts of the chair with the ends sewn into the cushion. Often the cushion was not attached, but loose.

The *wing chair*, usually imported, was another chair with a cushion. Until the mideighteenth century this chair, placed by the fire in the bed chamber, afforded protection from drafts. Its primary use was for a commode at that time, and it was not a parlor chair as we think of it today. The large squarish removable cushion served to hide the commode, and make the chair otherwise comfortable. Later in wealthy homes it was used without the commode and called an easy chair.

Upholstery

The early seventeenth-century Cromwellian-type chair, nailed with leather, sealskin, or serge—and for the wealthy, covered with velvet, plush, and other imported fabrics—was an early form of upholstery. Along with the aforementioned three-footed stool, it was undoubtedly imported. However, by the mideighteenth century, the American easy chair with its high winged back was "stuff-covered" and nailed in the same manner as the Cromwellian chair. Large-headed nails were used. Open armchairs were also upholstered in this manner. By the early or midnineteenth century the rural areas had simplified and unsophisti-

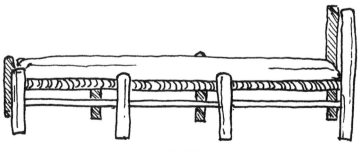

DAY BED

This New England country adaptation of the seventeenth-century day bed has a flag-woven bottom and a full-length cushion.

169

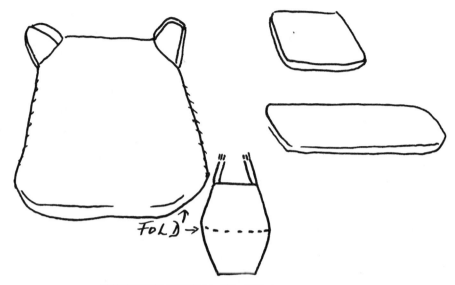

CUSHIONS SHAPED TO FIT CHAIR SEATS

Some were loose while others had tabs sewn into the pillow which looped around the rear posts of the chair. Thickness of the cushions averaged 1½-2 inches.

cated versions of the easy chair, and the sofa in a simple form had filled a special place along the wall in the parlor, if a family was lucky enough to own one. These were upholstered, having smooth backs that barely curved, if at all, and tight uncushioned seats. The arms were small, thin, and often awkward-looking. All were upholstered, with bared hand-hewn or turned wooden legs. Dyed linsey-woolsey, horsehair, and wool stuff were thought to be used for covering. Canvas or tow cloth was possibly used as a base.

WING CHAIR

The chair shown here was a country adaptation of the fashionable easy chair. It was made primarily of wood. Only the inside of the wings, arms, and cushion were stuffed and covered in fabric.

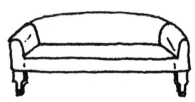

TIGHT-SEATED COUNTRY SOFA

This was for putting along the parlor wall. It is not very comfortable by twentieth-century standards, but it was a luxury for the rural American of the nineteenth century.

Slipcovers

Slipcovers were not uncommon to the wealthy. In fact, they were quite fashionable to cover and protect fine needlework or other elegant fabric and to cover upholstered fabric that was beginning to show signs of wear. These coverings were known as *loose covers* or *cases* (the word "casing" was usually applied to cushions). Covering several items in a room was not unusual, having been recorded as early as 1653 in Boston. Loose covers reached the height of fashion in the last half of the eighteenth century and the first half of the nineteenth century. For the wealthy, cotton twill stripes, patterned chintzes, silks, velvets, and serge were popular loose cover fabrics. Easy chairs were covered in loose covers so that they could be washed.

The *furniture check* of cotton or linen was also very popular for loose covering furnishings throughout the everyday bedroom (a lesser bedroom) in a wealthy household. Since checks had been traditional in rural Europe for generations, as can be seen in genre paintings and prints

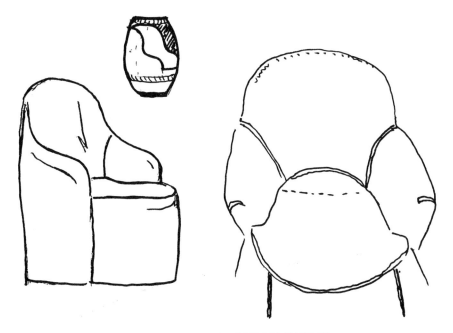

CHILD'S CHAIR CUT FROM BARREL

The slipcover shows the seams. It has a slight padding on the seat and down the front, and is slightly gathered over the top of the rounded back.

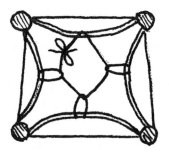

UNDERSIDE OF CHAIR SEAT,
SHOWING EDGE OF
SLIPCOVER

*Tape loops sewn into binding or
hem extend for string to pass through
and secure all sides.*

UNDERSIDE OF CHAIR SEAT,
SHOWING STRAIGHT
STRINGS FOR TYING

of seventeenth- and eighteenth-century Europe and England, it was not unexpected that rural America should find it natural to use checks in many ways regardless of the fashion. When woven at home, the various colors and sizes of checks were of single-ply closely set linen, most often in plain weave. Colors used rurally because of dyes available were medium or china blue, indigo, black, brown, and later, red, with white. Sizes of checks varied from $\frac{5}{16}$-inch to $1\frac{5}{8}$-inch, the $\frac{7}{8}$-inch to 1-inch being used frequently for large furniture. One of the most unusual loose covers found is illustrated on page 160. This blue and white home-woven checkered linen cover encases a unique barrel chair for a child. Loose covers were made mainly in rural areas for use on sofas or chairs. They were easily washed or removed "for company." Fitted closely to the shape of the furniture, they had neatly bound or turned edges. Incorporated in the turned hem were tape loops at the underside of the cover

UNDERSIDE OF CHAIR SEAT,
SHOWING NAILS

*Nails placed on bottom of chair seat frame
held slipcover when eyelet slipped over.*

in three places. The fourth side was sewn with tapes long enough to allow one end to thread through the three loops and tie at the fourth side. Sometimes there were just straight tapes or strings for tying.

Nails also may have been used on open arm chairs as a means of fastening the cover. Eyelet holes, cut and embroidered on the cover's lower edges, would be slipped over the nails for securing.

chapter 7

RUGS AND CARPETING

*T*HE EARLIEST USES of rugs were as table carpets and bed rugs (see chapters 3 and 4). Seventeenth-century inventories record the use of imported Turkish and oriental carpets for table covers. Bed rugs were listed in inventories in the seventeenth century and well into the eighteenth century in the context of bed furnishings, not for use on floors. By the mideighteenth century the wealthy in New England purchased the imported English- and French-manufactured copies of oriental rugs for floor use known as Turkey and Persia carpets. Also there were the English-made Wilton, Brussels, and Axminster carpets, as well as the Scotch ingrain carpets imported by the wealthy at this time. Later, in the nineteenth century, these were American-manufactured. But the use of floor rugs or carpets came very late to New England farming communities. There the concept of carpeting on the floor was not known until well into the nineteenth century. Country floors, in the seventeenth century and early eighteenth century, for the most part, were kept bare and unfinished, with only an occasional use of an animal hide, such as a bear or deer skin.

Many small one-room settlers' homes were built with niceties such as floors left for the future, after land had been cleared and crops planted. This tradition of beginning farming on a parcel of land with a one-room house, adding on as family size demanded and time would allow, continued in the upcountry far into the late eighteenth century. As late as 1805, Noah Blake wrote in his diary, as recorded in Eric Sloane's *Diary of an Early American Boy*: "March 26. We felled a fine oak and rolled it upon rails for spring seasoning. Mother is joyous at the thought of a good wood floor." They had been living a year in a one-room house with no floor. Women settlers, such as Noah's mother, knew they had to make do for a while with the hard earthen floor, pounded and swept every day. When visitors were expected at Christmas or another special holiday, the floor would be freshly swept and pounded. Then a scroll or decorative holiday design was drawn in with a stick to make a border. Such was "carpet" design in those days.

We in the twentieth century have lived with polished and carpeted floors. We live with conveniences such as cars and attached garages protecting us from the elements. Paved streets, driveways, and lawns near our houses keep our feet relatively clean. Living in an eighteenth-century farmhouse meant frequent steps out into a dirt barnyard, rain or shine, to tend livestock, milk cows, and feed geese and chickens, and heavy, dirty work in the fields. Throughout the seasons of New England's fickle weather, floors took a lot of rough abuse and needed frequent sweeping and sanding. Sand was the common method of cleaning the wide wooden floorboards. After scrubbing, the sand was swept away. Sometimes dry fresh sand was spread on the clean floor, then brushed or swept into scroll patterns or other designs in preparation for callers or some other special occasion.

In the eighteenth century a rug was pure luxury. In many country homes floors remained bare into the nineteenth century, with the exception of the "front room." If time and wool were available, the front room was carpeted with a handwoven rug, made at home or by an itinerant weaver. The front room, or parlor, as it was later called, was set aside from the traffic and chores of the day, awaiting the unexpected visitor, a ladies' gathering for tea, or a special family occasion. A multistriped woven wool carpet or a rag carpet would be made to cover the parlor floor. The hand-woven striped carpets were copies or adaptations of similar English manufactured carpets and were commonly in use by mid-nineteenth-century rural households.

Warp-faced Striped Carpeting

Handwoven warp-faced striped carpeting was first used after the Revolution, but as with other textile furnishings, it was slowly adopted in the rural areas. By the early to midnineteenth century warp-faced striped carpeting, along with other types of woven carpeting, was in common use rurally. It was adapted from imported English manufactured carpeting of similar style, as seen in English portrait paintings of the period. The designs of many-width stripes, narrow bars, and even checks were usually of two-ply wool—sometimes homespun, or combined with two-ply mill yarn, which was available in the early nineteenth century. Some originals show combinations of mill and homespun with a third yarn: cotton warping of stringlike weight. The various stripe designs were achieved by a clever yarn arrangement alternating colors in the lengthwise warp yarns. When the plain weave of the crosswise weft yarn was passed from side to side, the warp yarns created the stripe patterns and became the surface yarn on both sides of the carpeting in a warp-faced weave. The weft yarn was almost invisible, making the rug reversible. Being closely woven, it was smooth-surfaced and easy to clean. It also was very durable. The filler or weft yarn was usually heavy linen or sometimes (later), narrow strips of woolen cloth. The stripes were often designed cleverly so that when several woven panels were sewn side by side, the meeting of stripes made interesting and dramatic effects as a large carpet. Usually the carpets were finished with a narrow hem or cloth-bound; sometimes the warp ends were knotted in a simple fringe. Warp yarns of wool were dyed many colors. The earlier predominantly vege-

176

table dyes were softer. Later nineteenth-century woven rugs had brighter colors from purchased dyes and mill-dyed and mill-spun yarns.

Strips of carpeting were used also for stairways. The fashion of striped carpeting went even to very modest levels. Homes that were not able to have carpeting for stairs simply painted border stripes on the treads and risings to simulate woven carpet.

Matting

Straw and rush were also used for woolen striped rugs as weft. These rugs, however, were known as *matting*.

Another type of hand-loomed carpet or matting was made in the early nineteenth century and continued its popularity through the Victorian era, although imported during the later period. This was woven of linen warp, sometimes dyed, and had a rush, straw, or natural grass filler. It was known as *straw carpeting* or *straw matting*. This matting was used in summer in place of woolen carpeting.

Rag Rugs

Rag rugs were also a popular type of carpeting. These were very common and most easily made, requiring no special designing or weaving skill to turn out a very serviceable rug good for many years of wear. These hand-woven carpets utilized various pieces of clothing, sheeting, and blankets that had otherwise outlived their usefulness. Every scrap of cloth was saved, even lists, or strips of selvage cut from cloth. These were redyed, if necessary, and cut into narrow strips; then the strips were sewn together end on end and used as filler. The warps are most frequently found to be of factory-spun cotton, but some were of dyed linen, cotton, or wool, or combinations of these three. The setting, or spacing, of this warp could be considerably wider than the very close-set warp of the warp-faced woven striped carpeting. This allowed the filler to show. The dyed strips of cloth, woven in alternating or hit-or-miss fashion, made gaily colored rag rugs of considerable durability. Rag carpets were woven in lengthwise panels and sewn together.

References are many as to the weaving and the colorful practicality of rag carpets. Alice Morse Earle, writing about Narragansett, Rhode Island in 1898, states, "In Narragansett I know a score of old looms in good running order, though save in one instance, set only for weaving rag carpets; in many cases the owners, who do not make weaving a trade, will not 'start them up'. This [the rag carpet] is a long strip for a room in a cottage or farm house, so neighbors frequently join together in ordering these carpets, and in company send vast rolls of the filling, which is made of inch-wide strips of cloth of all colors and materials sewed in long strips." She goes on to say the rag carpeting technique was also used for the weaving of heavy silk-filled carpets hung in doorways: "Within a few years these old handlooms have been used for weaving rag portieres made of silk strips."

Samuel Goodrich wrote in *Recollections of a Lifetime*, published circa 1827 in Ridgefield, Connecticut: "Carpets were then [early 1800s] only known in a few families and were confined to the keeping room and parlor. They were all home-made, the warp consisting of woolen yarn and the woof of lists and old woolen cloth, cut into strips, and sewed together at the ends."

Rag rugs were made in great quantities by the itinerant weavers in the nineteenth century. The itinerant's loom would be set up with many yards of the ready warp and he would augment the supply of strips sewn together by the women with those of his own. The tradition has persisted, for even now small rag rugs can be found on country roadsides for sale.

Canvas Rugs or Floor Cloths

In the mideighteenth century the wealthy people along the seacoast were importing carpets from England, such as the Axminster, Wilton, and Brussels designs. They also followed the English vogue of using imported painted floor cloths, sometimes called canvas rugs, as well as manufactured carpets in their important rooms. This fashion in imported floor cloths filtered down to the rural New Englanders in the early nineteenth century because they were so practical, and they were adapted by ambitious New England housewives in their homes. The imported floor cloths and those manufactured here were made on wide looms, woven of hemp and tow canvas, and painted with copies of the designs on English-made Turkey carpets and Scottish ingrain carpets; the New Englander made her own yarn of homespun linen or cotton, wove it, sized it, and followed her recipe for painting, decorating, and glazing. Nina Fletcher Little quotes a statement made by Mary A. (Walkley) Beach of Stonington, Connecticut, circa 1828. "When I was four years old, I think, Mother spun and wove some linen cloth and had it nailed to the side of the barn and painted it herself for oil cloth. It did not cover the South room entirely, but did almost and saved scrubbing." These floor cloths proved very practical, especially on stairs and hallways, where they got a lot of wear. When the design on a cloth began to fade, it was repainted and glazed. The floor cloths were easily cleaned with a damp cloth and sometimes polished with milk, then rubbed dry. They could be left on the floor in winter with other rugs laid over them. The designs were usually geometrics with borders or copies of imported carpets. Eventually stenciling made the repetitious center motifs and borders more easily painted. Peddlers were known to have carried patterns. Itinerant house painters also painted new patterns on floor cloths.

As the nineteenth century progressed, rugs were not the luxury that they had been. Carpets, rugs, and matting were used increasingly in several rooms of the rural house.

Yarn-sewn Rug

Hooked rugs were of a later period than is widely thought. In fact, they were preceded in the early to midnineteenth century by the *yarn-sewn rug*. Using a needle with heavy yarn, the yarn was formed into loops on the top side of the handwoven linen backing by means of a running stitch. This is easily seen upon viewing the backing. This looping technique was similar to that used for making the early bed rug. The pile was sometimes cut, as well as left in uncut loops. The early yarn-sewn rugs were usually small, worked in very simple geometrics or floral designs similar to bed rugs. The foundation backing was often handwoven linen or coarse tow.

Hooked Rugs

Hooked Rugs, that followed soon after, were actually made with a hook to implement forming the loop. They were made generally on a burlap backing stretched over a frame. Most burlap-backed hooked rugs date from 1850 on, though handwoven backing was used prior to that date. The hooking material was strips of household fabrics, some homewoven and others purchased. Since a number of dyes were available by this date, the rugmaker could create bright, colorful designs of her choice. Yankee peddlers are known to have brought printed hooking designs to the rural areas beginning in the 1870s, but many floral, animal, and village scenes with simple borders were created by the housewife without the help of printed patterns. These are among the most charming and imaginative in design.

Braided Rugs

Braided rugs, often incorporating handwoven strips as well as other wools, were popular and made about the same time as hooked rugs, from 1850 on. They are still popular today.

An interesting rug was sewn from pieces of white fustian, black wool twill (now brown), and wide strips of blue wool twill. The twills are handwoven. It is unique in its design of alternating four- to five-inch strips of brown and medium blue twill. It is bordered with an appliquéd 1½-inch strip of white, and on each of the blue and brown strips are white appliquéd pieces in star, cross, and diamond shapes. One wonders if it may have been symbolic in its designs. It dates about 1790 and measures 6 feet 8 inches in length and 17¼ inches in width. The Essex Institute in Salem, Massachusetts displays this rug in a bed chamber setting.

BIBLIOGRAPHY

(*Note:* An asterisk before a book listing means that the book in question contains pattern drafts.)

BOOKS

Acomb, Evelyn M., trans. and ed. *The Revolutionary Journal of Baron Ludwig von Closen 1780–1783*. Chapel Hill: University of North Carolina Press, 1958.

Adrosko, Rita J. *Natural Dyes in the United States*. Washington, D.C.: Smithsonian Institution Press, 1968.

American Heritage editors. *American Heritage History of American Antiques from Revolution to Civil War, 1783–1860*. New York: Simon & Schuster for American Heritage Publishing Co., 1968.

*Atwater, Mary Meigs. *Summer and Winter Weaves, Then and Now*. Salt Lake City: published by the author, 1947.

*———. *The Shuttle-Craft Book of American Handweaving*. 7th printing. New York: Macmillan Co., 1966.

Austen, Jane. *Persuasion*. Boston: Little, Brown & Co., 1903.

Baker, Muriel L. *A Handbook of American Crewel Embroidery*. Rutland, Vt.: Charles E. Tuttle Co., 1966.

Batchellor, Albert Stillman, and Hammond, Otis G., eds. *Probate Records of the Province of New Hampshire*. State and Provincial Papers Series, vols. 1–4. Concord, N.H.: Rumford Printing Co., 1907–1935.

Bissell, Charles S. *Antique Furniture in Suffield, Connecticut, 1670–1835*. The Connecticut Historical Society and The Suffield Historical Society, 1956.

*Black, Mary E. *Key to Weaving*. Rev. ed. Milwaukee: Bruce Publishing Co., 1945.

Briggs, Martin. *The Homes of the Pilgrim Fathers in England and America, 1620–1685*. London and New York: Oxford University Press, 1932.

Bronson, J., and Bronson, R. *The Domestic Manufacturer's Assistant*. Utica, N.Y.: William Williams, 1817.

Bullock, Orin M., Jr. *The Restoration Manual*. 2d ed. Norwalk, Conn.: Silvermine Publishing, 1971.

Callister, J. Herbert, and Warren, William L. *Bed Ruggs: 1722–1833*. Hartford, Conn.: Wadsworth Atheneum, 1972.

Chamberlain, Samuel, and Chamberlain, Narcissa. *The Chamberlain Selection of New England Rooms 1639–1863*. New York: Hastings House, 1972.

Chamberlain, Samuel, and Flynt, Henry N. *Historic Deerfield: Houses and Interiors*. Rev. ed. New York: Hastings House, 1972.

Channing, Marion L. *Textile Tools of Colonial Times*. 2d ed. Marion, Mass.: The Channings, 1971.

————. *The Magic of Spinning*. Marion, Mass.: The Channings, 1971.

Christensen, Erwin O. *The Index of American Design*. New York: Macmillan Co. for the National Gallery of Art, Smithsonian Institution, Washington, D.C., 1950.

Cooper, Grace Rogers. *The Copp Family Textiles*. Washington, D.C.: Smithsonian Institution Press, 1971.

Cummings, Abbott Lowell. *Architecture in Early New England*. Sturbridge, Mass.: Old Sturbridge Village, 1958.

————. *Bed Hangings*. Boston: Society for Preservation of New England Antiquities, 1961.

————. *Rural Household Inventories*.* Boston: Society for Preservation of New England Antiquities, 1964.

Darisch, Mildred. *Early American Hand-Woven Coverlets*. Chicago: The Art Institute, 1946.

Davidson, Mary Frances. *The Dye Pot*. Gatlinburg, Tenn.: published by the author, 1950.

Davis, Mildred J. *Early American Embroidery Designs*. New York: Crown Publishers, 1969.

* Including Essex, Middlesex, and Suffolk counties in Massachusetts.

*Davison, Marguerite Porter. *A Handweaver's Pattern Book*. 4th printing. Swarthmore, Pa.: published by the author, 1955.

Dickens, Charles. *American Notes*. London: MacMillan & Co., 1893.

Dolan, J. R. *The Yankee Peddlers of Early America*. New York: Clarkson N. Potter, 1964.

Dow, George Francis. *Everyday Life in the Massachusetts Bay Colony*. New York: B. Blom, 1967.

————. *The Arts and Crafts in New England, 1704–1775*. Topsfield, Mass.: Wayside Press, 1927.

————. *Two Centuries of Travel in Essex County, Massachusetts*. Topsfield, Mass.: Perkins Press, 1931.

Downs, Joseph. *American Furniture, Queen Anne and Chippendale Periods*. New York: Macmillan Co., 1952.

Earle, Alice Morse. *In Old Narragansett, Romances and Realities*. New York: Charles Scribner's Sons, 1898.

————. *Homelife in Colonial Days*. New York: Macmillan Co., 1898.

Eaton, Allen H. *Handicrafts in New England*. New York: Harper Bros., 1949.

————. *Handicrafts of the Southern Highlands*. New York: Russell Sage Foundation, 1937.

Edwin, James E. Thorold Rogers. *The Story of Holland*. New York: G. P. Putnam's Sons, 1892.

Fennelly, Catherine. *Life in an Old New England Country Village*. Sturbridge, Mass.: Old Sturbridge Village, 1969.

————. *The Garb of Country New Englanders, 1790–1840*. Sturbridge, Mass.: Old Sturbridge Village, 1966.

————. *The New England Village Scene: 1800*. Sturbridge, Mass.: Old Sturbridge Village, 1955.

Flexner, James T. *American Paintings: First Flowers of Our Wilderness*. Boston: Houghton Mifflin Co., 1954.

Forster, John. *The Life of Charles Dickens*. London: J. M. Dent & Sons, 1927.

*Gallagher, Constance. *Linen Heirlooms*. Newton Centre, Mass.: Charles T. Branford Co., 1971.

Gates, Paul W. *The Farmer's Age: Agriculture, 1815–1860*. The Economic History of the United States, vol. 3. New York: Harper & Row, 1960.

Glassie, Henry. *Pattern in the Material Folk Culture of the Eastern United States*. Folklore and Folklife Series. Philadelphia: University of Pennsylvania Press, 1971.

Gowans, Alan. *Images of American Living*. Philadelphia: J. B. Lippincott Co., 1964.

Hall, Eliza Calvert. *A Book of Handwoven Coverlets*. Rutland, Vt.: Charles E. Tuttle Co., 1966.

Hands That Built New Hampshire: Spinning and Weaving in New Hampshire. WPA Writers' Program. Brattleboro, Vt.: Stephen Daye Press, 1940.

Harbeson, Georgiana Brown. *American Needlework.* New York: Bonanza Books, 1938.

Hartley, Dorothy, and Elliot, Margaret. *Life and Work of the People of England.* Vols. 2 and 3. New York: G. P. Putnam's Sons, 1926.

Hechtlinger, Adelaide. *American Quilts, Quilting, and Patchwork: The Complete Book of History and Technique.* An Early American Society Book. Harrisburg, Pa.: Stackpole Books, 1974.

Hedlund, Catherine A. *A Primer of New England Crewel Embroidery.* 2d ed. Sturbridge, Mass.: Old Sturbridge Village, 1967.

Heritage Foundation. *Early American Embroideries in Deerfield.* Deerfield, Mass.: Heritage Foundation, 1963.

Hess, Katherine. *Textile Fibres and Their Use.* 6th ed. Philadelphia: J. B. Lippincott Co., 1958.

Hitchcock, Enos. *The Farmer's Friend, or the History of Mr. Charles Worthy.* Boston: I. Thomas and E. T. Andrews, 1793.

Howells, John Mead. "The Homes of the Pilgrim Fathers in England and America (1620–1685)." In *Lost Examples of Colonial Architecture.* 1930–1935. Reprint. New York: Dover Publications, 1963.

Isham, Norman, and Brown, Albert. *Early Connecticut Houses.* New York: Dover Publications, 1900.

Iverson, Marion Day. *The American Chair, 1630–1890.* New York and Philadelphia: Hastings House, 1957.

Kettell, Russell Hawes. *Early American Rooms, 1650–1858.* New York: Dover Publications, 1967.

Kovel, Ralph M., and Kovel, Terry M. *American Country Furniture, 1780–1875.* 7th printing. New York: Crown Publishers, 1972.

Life editors. *America's Arts and Skills.* New York: E. P. Dutton & Co., 1957.

Lippman, Jean. *Rufus Porter, Yankee Pioneer.* New York: C. N. Potter, 1968.

Little, Frances. *Early American Textiles.* New York and London: Century Co., 1931.

Little, Nina Fletcher. *Abby Aldrich Rockefeller Folk Art Collection.* 1st ed. Boston: Little, Brown & Co., 1957.

————. *Floor Coverings in New England Before 1850.* Sturbridge, Mass.: Old Sturbridge Village, 1967.

McLanathan, Richard. *American Tradition in the Arts.* New York: Harcourt, Brace & World, 1969.

Montgomery, Florence. *Printed Textiles, English and American Cottons and Linens, 1700–1850.* New York: Viking Press, 1970.

Murphy, John. *A Treatise on the Art of Weaving.* Glasgow and Edinburgh:

Blackie, Fullerton & Co., Glasgow, and Archibald Fullerton & Co., Edinburgh, 1827.

*Nesbit, H. *Grammar of Textile Design.* 3d ed. Bombay: Russi J. Taraporevala for D. B. Taraporevala Sons & Co., 1961.

Nettels, Curtis P. *The Emergence of a National Economy, 1775–1850.* The Economic History of the United States, vol. 2. New York: Harper & Row, 1962.

Nutting, Wallace. *Furniture Treasury.* Vols. 1 and 2. 10th ed. New York: Macmillan Co., 1972.

*Oelsner, G. H. *A Handbook of Weaves.* 1915. Reprint. New York: Dover Publications, 1952.

Parslow, Virginia D. *Weaving and Dyeing Process in Early New York.* Cooperstown, N.Y.: The Farmer's Museum, 1949.

Peto, Florence. *American Quilts and Coverlets.* New York: Chanticleer Press, 1949.

Pratt, Richard. *A Treasury of Early American Homes.* New York: McGraw-Hill Book Co., 1949.

Pratt, Richard, and Pratt, Dorothy. *The Second Treasury of Early American Homes.* New York: Hawthorn Books, 1954.

Preston, Paula Sampson. *Printed Cottons at Old Sturbridge Village.* Sturbridge, Mass.: Old Sturbridge Village, 1969.

Probate Records of Essex County, Massachusetts. Vols. 1–3. Salem, Mass.: Essex Institute, 1916–1920.

Quennell, Marjorie, and Quennell, G. H. B. *A History of Everyday Things in England.* Vol. 2, 1500–1799, and vol. 3, 1733–1851. 6th ed. London: B. T. Batsford, 1954.

Robinson, Stuart. *A History of Dyed Textiles.* Cambridge, Mass.: MIT Press, 1969.

Rogers, Meyric R. *American Interior Design: The Traditions and Development of Domestic Design from Colonial Times to the Present.* Chicago: The Art Institute, 1947.

Safford, Carleton L., and Bishop, Robert. *America's Quilts and Coverlets.* New York: E. P. Dutton & Co., 1972.

Schwartz, Marvin D. *American Interiors 1675–1885.* New York: Brooklyn Museum, 1968.

Sloane, Eric. *Diary of an Early American Boy: Noah Blake 1805.* New York: Wilfred Funk, 1962.

Sprackling, Helen. *Customs on the Table Top.* Sturbridge, Mass.: Old Sturbridge Village, 1958.

Swygert, Mrs. Luther M., ed. *Heirlooms from Old Looms.* Chicago and Crawfordsville, Ind.: R. R. Donnelley & Sons for Colonial Coverlet Guild of America, 1955.

*Tidball, Harriet. *The Weaver's Book.* New York: Macmillan Co., 1961.

*———. *Thomas Jackson, Weaver.* Lansing, Mich.: The Shuttle Craft Guild, 1964.

van Wagenen, Jared, Jr. *The Golden Age of Homespun*. Ithaca, N.Y.: Cornell University Press, 1953.

Winchester, Alice, and the staff of *Antiques* magazine, eds. *The Antiques Treasury of Furniture and Other Decorative Arts*. New York: E. P. Dutton & Co., 1959.

*Young, Helen D. *Heritage Linens Interpreted in Profile*. North Hanover, Mass.: published by the author, 1957.

ARTICLES

Antiques editors. "The Textiles." *Antiques*, September 1956 (Deerfield Issue).

Bailey, Richard B. "Pilgrim Possessions 1620–1640." *Antiques*, March 1952.

Carlisle, Lillian Baker. "The Stencil House at Shelburne Museum." *Antiques*, June 1959.

Comstock, Helen. "Chronology of Crafts." *Antiques*, October 1959.

———. "Directory of Source Books." *Antiques*, August 1960.

———. "18th Century Floor Cloths." *Antiques*, January 1955.

Cummin, Hazel E. "What Was Dimity in 1790?" *Antiques*, July 1940.

———. "Colonial Dimities Checked and Diapered." *Antiques*, September 1940.

———. "Tammies and Durants." *Antiques*, September 1941.

Cummings, Abbott Lowell. "Connecticut Homespun." *Antiques*, September 1954.

———. "Antiques at Old Sturbridge Village: The Buildings." *Antiques*, September 1955.

———. "The Society's Collections: Library and Photographs." *Antiques*, May 1960 (Society for the Preservation of New England Antiquities Issue).

Davison, Mildred. "Hand-woven Coverlets in the Art Institute of Chicago." *Antiques*, May 1970.

Deetz, James. "The Reality of the Pilgrim Fathers." *Natural History*, November 1969.

Downs, Joseph, and Winchester, Alice. "The First Colonial Century" and "The Queen Anne Period." *Antiques*, November 1951 (Winterthur Issue).

Dudley, W. P. "History in Houses: The Garrison House, Exeter, New Hampshire." *Antiques*, August 1960.

Evans, Mary. "American Treasury, A Wing Full of Glory." *American Home*, December 1970.

Fennelly, Catherine. "Antiques at Old Sturbridge Village: Textiles and Costumes." *Antiques*, September 1955.

Fisher Scientific Co., Pittsburgh, Pa. "No Woolgathering Here." *The Laboratory* 34, no. 4.

Garrett, Wendell D. "Living with Antiques: The Connecticut Home of Mary Allis." *Antiques*, November 1969.

Gibson, Gerald G. "Henry Ford's Greenfield Village." *Antiques*, September 1959 (Henry Ford Museum Issue).

Giffen, Jane C. "Household Textiles, a Review." *Historical New Hampshire* 22, no. 4 (1971).

Inman, Pauline. "House Furnishings of a Vermont Family." *Antiques*, August 1969.

Iverson, Marion Day. "Bed Rugs in Colonial America." *Antiques*, January 1964.

———. "Color in Pilgrim and Puritan Dress." *Antiques*, March 1952.

———. "Slipcovers of Past Centuries." *Antiques*, October 1951.

———. "Table Linen in Colonial America." *Antiques*, November 1959.

Jones, Louis C. "The Cooperstown Complex." *Antiques*, February 1959 (Cooperstown Issue).

Ketcham, Howard. "The Romance of Color." *American Fabrics*, Autumn 1952.

Kimball, Fiske, and Kimball, Marie. "Jefferson's Curtains at Monticello." *Antiques*, October 1947.

Lanier, Mildred B. "The Textile Furnishings." *Antiques*, January 1969 (Williamsburg Issue).

Linton, George. "Where Did It Come From?" *American Fabrics*, Autumn 1952.

Little, Nina Fletcher. "An Approach to Furnishing." *Antiques*, July 1956.

———. "Livery Cupboards in New England." *Antiques*, December 1963.

———. "The General Salem Towne House at Old Sturbridge Village." *Antiques*, April 1959.

———. "The House of Tristram Coffin, Jr." *Antiques*, May 1960.

———. "The Painted Decoration." *Antiques*, February 1959 (Cooperstown Issue).

MacFarlane, Janet R. "The Lippett Homestead." *Antiques*, August 1953.

Mailey, Jean. "Printed Textiles in America." *Antiques*, May 1956.

Munier, Margaret B. "Antiques at Old Sturbridge Village: The Furniture." *Antiques*, September 1955.

Palmer, Frederic. "The Hemsted House." *Antiques*, February 1950.

Pariseau, George E. "Weaver Rose of Rhode Island 1839–1913." *Handweaver and Craftsman*, Winter 1954–55.

Parslow, Virginia D. "The Textiles." *Antiques*, February 1959 (Cooperstown Issue).

Peto, Florence. "A Textile Discovery." *Antiques*, August 1953.

Preston, Paula Sampson. "Printed and Painted Cottons." *Antiques*, October 1969.

Rogers, Meyric R. "Wool-on-Wool Coverlet." *Antiques*, July 1958.

Schwartz, Esther I. "Early Commercial Weaving in Paterson." *Antiques*, October 1958.

Scott, Kenneth. "Advertising Woodcuts in Colonial Newspapers." *Antiques*, February 1955.

Shaffer, Sandra C. "Sewing Tools in the Collection of Colonial Williamsburg." *Antiques*, August 1973.

Snow, Barbara. "History in Houses." *Antiques*, January 1957.

Spinney, Frank O. "Country Furniture." *Antiques*, August 1953.

Vaughan, Malcolm. "Seventeenth Century and Queen Anne Furniture in Mrs. Garver's Collection." *Antiques*, December 1955.

Winchester, Alice. "Living with Antiques, Gogswell's Grant, the Essex County Home of Mr. and Mrs. Bertram K. Little." *Antiques*, February 1969.

————. "Longfellow's Wayside Inn." *Antiques*, August 1958.

————. "Period Rooms for New Hampshire." *Antiques*, December 1958.

————. "The Prentis House at the Shelburne Museum." *Antiques*, May 1957.

Wolfe, Ruth. "When Art Was a Household Word." *Ms.*, February 1974.

MANUSCRIPT MATERIAL

Plymouth, Mass. Plimouth Plantation Research Library. "Plimouth Colony Wills." Records of the Plimouth County Registry of Deeds from 1633 to 1750.

Salem, Mass. Essex Institute. "Fabrics and Styles of Colonial Window Hangings as Revealed Through Boston and Salem Records 1700–1760." Thesis by Anna Brightman.

PUBLIC DOCUMENTS

Barnstable County, Mass. Probate Office. "Inventory and Appraisal of Estate of Prince Gifford Late of Falmouth—February 16, 1804."

INDEX

(*Note:* Page numbers in italics refer to illustrations.)

189